SCANDALS

STORIES OF PSYCHIC CINDY

SCANDALS

STORIES OF PSYCHIC CINDY

CYNTHIA TREGLIA

WRITTEN BY

RAFAEL GORDIAN

TABLE OF CONTENTS

Dedication

To all my hundreds of clients who have been inspirational. My service continues to grow in many ways that I never dreamed possible. Not only have my clients inspired me, but they have given me the courage as a single mom to start Ctregs (www.ctregs.com). In addition, Danielle Curcio, Ctregs' fashion designer (www.designsbydanni.com), and Thomas Wallace, Ctregs' jewelry and artist (www.twallacedesign.com): There are no words strong enough to show my appreciation to the two of you. You both have been with me from the beginning through it all and have shown loyalty. I love you both unconditionally.

To my son, David, and daughter, Jessica, who remind me every day how wonderful it is to be a parent. I thank them for their patience in sharing me with my clients. I'm sure it isn't easy having a psychic as a mother. To my niece Ashley, who reminds me what it was like to be young.

To my personal friends (they know who they are): I thank them for good times, special moments, and countless bottles of Pinot Grigio. My final thoughts go to my mother and sister. My sister, Susan, has always been there for me through it all. Thank you, sis, you're the greatest! I wouldn't be the woman I am today without my mother, Dorothy (who is a breast cancer survivor). I thank you for all you have done and the love you share. I love you, Mom.

Rafael Gordian, you took my words and my ideas and creations and put them into the best-ever words! Thanks for bringing *Scandals: Stories of Psychic Cindy* to life.

Introduction

This book is based on actual events in my clients' lives. Their names have been changed to protect their privacy. All psychic readings are private and confidential. I decided to write this book because I needed to share my clients' real-life experiences. Sharing these real-life stories not only proved to be therapeutic; it became a collection of human emotions, pain, as well as fears that needed to be shared. By sharing these experiences it is my desire that my clients will draw a new sense of commonality and awareness. It is my hope that readers will experience my clients' lives as they struggle to find their place in everyday society.

My clients come from all walks of life. They are lawyers, doctors, teachers, nurses, factory workers, waitresses, exotic dancers, carpenters, cooks, and more. No matter where my clients come from, they all share something in common: They need to know what it takes to fix their lives and continue on a better path than the one they have chosen. This need to know is a basic desire, not only of my clients' but of everyone. Sometimes my clients may feel their lives are out of control, but with some spiritual and emotional guidance they are able to adapt to their changing needs.

Readers will experience a snapshot of the lives of the many clients who come through my office. The journey of human lives is always bound by grief and triumph. These stories can be tragic, as well as uplifting. They all, however, end with the truth of the matter. They were put together to entertain you as well. The stories will leave you wanting to know more about the private lives of these clients.

CHAPTER ONE
THE PLEDGE

Oral sex was never quite normal with Jethro. His favorite position during sex was to lie on his back with his full military uniform on, while I sat on top of him with my bush in his face. While eating me out, Jethro made me recite the Pledge of Allegiance. The more he wiggled his tongue, the less I was able to recite the Pledge and began losing my place. This was a big turn-on for him. He bet me that I would never be able to finish the Pledge of Allegiance.

ANNIE: "I pledge of allegiance to the Flag of the United States of America. I pledge allegiance to the flag, and to the Republic for which it stands... Invisible...

JETHRO paused his carnal activity to say: "No, not invisible, indivisible."

ANNIE: "Damn it, Jethro, just eat me."

To this day Annie has never been able to finish the Pledge of Allegiance.
FADE TO FULL STORY BELOW

THE OTHER WOMAN

They call me Annie. I am fifty-two years old and have four kids. The first time I met Jethro, I was unaware that he was married, and that he lived down South. This six-foot-tall blond redneck dazzled me with his scratchy voice and charming manners. He was every bit as country as a chicken coop. He knew how to draw you in to his world. It was almost like he got a thrill out of it. Jethro is an active military sergeant and always made sure that everyone he met knew his status. He always kept his uniform neat and pressed. His shoes always had that spit-shine to them.

One of Jethro's favorite hobbies is watching porn. If you wanted to know what sex is like with Jethro, it depends on which movie he saw. This may explain his sexual behavior, but couldn't explain why he has no morals. I asked him on many occasions about his childhood. He didn't like talking about his past, except to say that he grew up poor.

I knew that Jethro had other women in his life. His one-night stands never bothered me until now. I was building up my own business and wanted to start stabilizing my life. I wanted to share my achievements with someone who was close to me. My advisor psychic, Cindy, advised me to focus on getting my business started instead of "Jet," as she liked to call him.

Three months after we started dating, I found out Jethro was married. As much as it hurt me, I did not care because she was living down in North Carolina. At that time I was desperate for affection and the distance between New York and North Carolina is so wide that it was easy to ignore Jethro's other life.

As far as I was concerned, Jethro was mine, and belonged to me only. I kept having these crazy dreams about Jethro and the other woman. Once I dreamed that I confronted Jethro in front of the other woman to make a decision; it would be either me or her. Every time Jethro was about to answer, I would wake up in a cold sweat.

The feeling that there was another woman was overwhelming to me. Once I called Jethro's house and impersonated a telemarketer. This enabled me to obtain his wife's name and e-mail address. Now I had the name "Betty" but had no idea what she looked like. I was so desperate about Jethro that I sent photos of me and Jethro attached to e-mails to Betty. My moments of desperation came in waves of madness. These waves of madness started to get longer and more intense over time. It was as if I had a little devil sitting on my shoulder sticking me with a pitchfork.

This seems to surface with no warning. In one of these waves, I called Betty and told her that Jethro expressed his undying love to me. Jethro's first response was to shut down his phone. I decided to call Jethro on his cell phone.

JETHRO: "Are you out of your f@#king mind calling my wife!!!? What's the matter with you?"

ANNIE: "You're driving me to—
PHONE GOES DEAD.

Since Jethro would not take my calls, I decided to pay him a visit. Jethro told me that I was setting out to destroy him. He could not believe how far I would go for him. I decided to seek some comfort by meeting with my advisor, Psychic Cindy.

Because of Psychic Cindy's open-door policy, Annie seeks advice from Cindy at all hours of the day. Psychic Cindy is overwhelmed by Annie's round-the-clock reach to her because Annie is looking at Cindy as her therapist. Cindy takes great caution about her role and advice to Annie during this critical time. She hesitates to get between Annie and Jethro.

OFFICE OF PSYCHIC CINDY 10:00 A.M. FRIDAY MORNING

Psychic Cindy with her Assistant, Bebe

PSYCHIC CINDY: "Are you serious?"

ASSISTANT BEBE: "I'm serious. She told me she should be first because she has an emergency."

PSYCHIC CINDY: "What kind of emergency?"

ASSISTANT BEBE: "She wouldn't tell me. I told her there's no smoking in the waiting room. She looked at me like I was speaking a different language. She got up from her seat and walked over to my desk. Then she took a big drag on her cigarette and exhaled smoke in my face."

PSYCHIC CINDY: "It's okay, Bebe. I'll take care of her."

Psychic Cindy opens her door to her office. Annie is sitting down on the lounge chair with her feet up.

PSYCHIC CINDY: "I'm so glad that you made yourself at home. Okay, Annie, what's going on?"

ANNIE: "Cindy, I didn't come here for a reading. Is it okay if I just vent?"

PSYCHIC CINDY: "Sure, Annie. Be my guest. I'm all ears."

ANNIE: "Cindy, I don't get it. I really don't know why this is happening."

PSYCHIC CINDY: "Why, what happened?"

ANNIE: "I don't know why Jethro would stay with that chick. That freaking hillbilly redneck!"

PSYCHIC CINDY: "Is that why you blew smoke in my secretary's face?"

ANNIE: "She just aggravated the shit out of me. Walking around with her tight-ass body. Twenty years ago I could run circles around her!"

3

PSYCHIC CINDY: "Calm down. Jethro loves you, but you're going to scare him away."

Annie reaches in her purse for a bottle of pills, shaking nervously.

PSYCHIC CINDY: "What's that?"

ANNIE: "It's for the pain in my arm."

PSYCHIC CINDY: "Vicodin? Are you out of your mind? That is very addictive. Why are you doing this to yourself?"

ANNIE: "I wake up with these headaches. Think I'm having a breakdown."

PSYCHIC CINDY: "I told you before; don't contact Jethro for three weeks. Let him call you. Did you even last the three weeks?"

ANNIE: "Four hours."

PSYCHIC CINDY: "Four hours? You must be joking."

ANNIE: "He called me. He calls me all the time to tell me he loves me. It's because of my magic book."

PSYCHIC CINDY: "What 'magic book'? What the hell are you talking about?"

ANNIE: "I bought this spell book. It came with a guarantee. It has spells in it that you can put on someone."

PSYCHIC CINDY: "Really? What kind of spells?"

ANNIE: "My kind of spells."

PSYCHIC CINDY: "You're killing me. What kind is your kind? What the hell would make you want to put a spell on Jethro, of all people? You already have his heart."

ANNIE: "Well, he's calling me, no?"

PSYCHIC CINDY: "Okay, Annie, calm down."

Annie reaches for and pulls a fresh cigarette out of her purse.

ANNIE: "And that Betty bitch, I got something for her."

PSYCHIC CINDY: "You're not thinking what I think you're thinking of doing?"

ANNIE: "I went online and saw this article on how to break up a marriage."

4

PSYCHIC CINDY: "Oh, my God! You did what?" "No, you didn't"

ANNIE: "Yes, I did. It says that there has to be a full moon, and you use a chicken heart."

PSYCHIC CINDY: "You bought a chicken heart? Are you out of your mind?"

ANNIE: "Yep, and drawing stick figures of a man and a woman on paper. I placed the chicken heart on the woman figure and stabbed it."

PSYCHIC CINDY: "Okay, Annie, enough. I don't want to entertain this any further."

ANNIE: "What about my candles?"

PSYCHIC CINDY: "What candles?"

ANNIE: "I bought some candles at the botanical for Jethro."

PSYCHIC CINDY: "Now I know you're shot."

ANNIE: "I bought black candles for magic spells. Can you help me with this one?"

PSYCHIC CINDY: "Now, Annie, you ought to know better than that. Black magic spells—you have to be careful. If not done right, it could come back to you times three. The dark side is very powerful, not something I promote. You're on your own with that one, love. Sorry. Be careful is all I can tell you, since you're not experienced with the spiritual world. Now I'll be dreaming of chicken hearts tonight. And stick figures. Thanks!"

ANNIE: "I can't allow that bitch to control my Jethro."

PSYCHIC CINDY: "*Your* Jethro? What do you mean by 'your Jethro'? He's a married man."

ANNIE: "He tells me he loves me, not her."

PSYCHIC CINDY: "Yes, but at the end of the day, he always goes back to her."

ANNIE: "Maybe now, but that's about to change."

PSYCHIC CINDY: "Really?"

Meanwhile, Jethro is up to no good. Jethro is worried that Annie may be losing interest in him. Most of all he fears that she may find someone else. He decides to do something about this.

5

At Juanita's Botanica in upper Manhattan, a geeky-looking redneck sticks out like a sore thumb in a predominantly Dominican neighborhood.

The chime on the door gives Jethro's entrance away. Any effort to enter the store unnoticed quickly vanishes.

OWNER JUANITA: "Buenos Días, señor. Can I help you?"

JETHRO: "Hello."

JUANITA: "Is there something particular you're looking for?"

JETHRO: "Just looking around for now."

Jethro walks around and his eyes scan the stock shelves of candles, statue, incense, and various formulas and tools of the trade. He knows what he wants but hasn't spotted it yet. He finally gets tired of looking and gets the nerve to ask.

JETHRO: "Do you carry any dolls?"

JUANITA: "Dolls for decoration, or for spells?"

JETHRO: "It's for my daughter. She is doing a term paper on voodoo. I think she prefers the one for spells."

JUANITA: "I have two kinds. Are you looking for the female or the male doll?"

JETHRO: "Maybe I should take both. Yeah, how about I take both of them?"

JUANITA: "That will be fifteen dollars for the male and ten dollars for the female doll. Does your daughter know how powerful these dolls can be? Does she know that these dolls can impair a person's life? I have to remind you they are dolls for the purpose of *trabajo*."

JETHRO: "What does that mean, *trabajo*?"

JUANITA: "Dolls for the purpose of spells."

Jethro tries to play it off like he's a completely ignorant redneck. He pretends to have no idea of what Juanita is saying. The truth is he's analyzing everything she says.

JETHRO: "I think so; she is going to make a presentation to her class. It might be helpful to be as authentic as possible."

JUANITA: "I have a great book of spells. It's thirty-five dollars. Would you like to see it?"

JETHRO: "That sounds good. I'd like to see it."

Juanita goes to the back of the store and returns in three minutes. She hands Jethro a book called *Black Magic Darkness.*

Jethro examines the book and is crazed by what he sees: two dolls buried in a cemetery.

JETHRO: "I'll take it."

Juanita knows these things aren't really for Jethro's daughter, but goes along with him for the sale.

JUANITA: "I hope your daughter is very happy with your purchase for her."

JETHRO: "Oh, she's going to be ecstatic. Thank you very much."

As Jethro leaves Juanita's Botanica, he wears a devious smile. He holds on tightly to his shopping bag full of voodoo arsenal. He tickles the wind chime on the door with his finger on his way out.

To keep Annie from finding his voodoo tools, Jethro stashes everything in the trunk of his car. While Jethro is in New York, he spends some time with her. According to the instruction in the magic book, Jethro needs a strand of Annie's hair. He manages to pick up several strands from the passenger seat in his car. Jethro stuffs the hair in a sandwich baggie and pockets it.

Now that Jethro has everything he needs for the spell, he decides to make a trip down South. He tells Annie he has to leave to attend a three-week seminar at the base. On his way down South, Jethro pulls the book out of the shopping bag and lays it down on the passenger seat.

SEVERAL DAYS LATER ON US ROUTE 95, about 8 p.m.

Jethro is driving home and is listening to his favorite station, DC 101, when he hears a song entitled "I Put a Spell on You" by Screaming Jay Hawkins. He begins to laugh and choke at the same time.

Three minutes later Jethro is pulled over by Washington DC state troopers.

While one of the troopers remains in the car, the other walks over to Jethro's car. The trooper scans the interior of the car with his flashlight and catches a glimpse of a book on the passenger seat. The book is faced up and he notices the title on the cover: *Black Magic Darkness.* The trooper also notices that Jethro is dressed up in a military uniform.

TROOPER JONES: "License, registration, and insurance card."

JETHRO: "Was I going too fast?"

TROOPER JONES: "Are you active military?"

JETHRO: "Right out of Fort Myers."

The trooper shines the flashlight in Jethro's face for a moment.

TROOPER JONES: "Do any drinking tonight?"

JETHRO: "No, sir."

TROOPER JONES: "If I ask you to take a Breathalyzer test, will you pass it?"

JETHRO: "Absolutely."

TROOPER JONES: "I'll be right back."

The trooper returns to his car to consult with the other officer and scan Jethro's documents.

TROOPER KENNY: "What's it look like, Jones?"

TROOPER JONES: "Let's punch his data in and find out."

Five minutes later…

TROOPER KENNY: "So far, he's coming up clean."

Trooper Jones returns to Jethro, who is smoking his third cigarette.

TROOPER JONES: "Here are your documents, Mr. Orrick. The reason I pulled you over is because you were driving over the white line."

JETHRO: "Sorry, Officer, I didn't realize how tired I am."

TROOPER JONES: "Where are you headed?"

JETHRO: "North Carolina."

TROOPER JONES: "You need your rest for a trip like that. If you have to pull over and sleep, it's fine by us. Oh, and by the way…"

JETHRO: "Yes?"

TROOPER JONES: "It's easier and safer to read a book when you're not driving." Jethro feels a little embarrassed, but decides it's best if he remains silent.

TROOPER JONES: "You have a safe and pleasant trip."

After twenty or so miles Jethro decides to take the trooper's advice, and pulls over to rest. He grabs the book and continues to read where he left off before he was pulled over.

JETHRO: "Smart ass cop, how the hell did he know I was reading? What a jerk#*f."

Ten miles away from home, Jethro makes a stop at a local cemetery.

He takes advantage of this night because there's a full moon. It's just about midnight, and Jethro assumes that no one else is around. Unknown to him, the overnight caretaker is making his rounds.

He leaves the car on and heads for a group of headstones with the two dolls, a strand of Annie's hair, and one of his socks. Under his other arm is a shovel. According to the directions in the book, he must begin his spell at midnight.

Meanwhile the graveyard caretaker, Igor, has spotted the headlights from the car. Igor is nosy and heads toward the light and noise that he hears. Igor sees Jethro digging and thinks Jethro is grave-robbing. Because the graveyard is closed after 7 p.m., Igor knows all graveyard workers have gone for the day. Igor decides he better call the police.

Jethro begins to dig a hole to bury the dolls in. According to the directions in the book, he must attach a strand of Annie's hair to the female doll. The sock is put on the male doll. This will bind him and Annie together for life. The final touches are the burial of the dolls.

Before the burial of the dolls, Jethro recites a chant that must be said:

"Spirit of the Dead,
"I need you,
"I want you.
"Bind Annie back,
"Bind Annie back to me.
"I will give you a cup of rum and a cigar as an offering."

Not knowing what to expect, the police arrive and work their way up to Jethro quietly. They are stunned by what they see and hear. It takes a moment for the police to shake off what they see.

As Jethro is chanting out loud, a blinding light suddenly appears in his face. Jethro looks up and sees two cops, one of them holding a flashlight directed at him.

POLICE OFFICER COLE: "Okay, mister, party's over. Get up nice and slow."

JETHRO: "I can't stop now. It will break the spell."

POLICE OFFICER COLE: "Mister, you have two seconds to comply."

Jethro ignores the cops and continues to chant:

"Bind Annie to me.

"Bind Annie only to me."

Officer Cole jumps on Jethro, knocking him to the ground. He places his knee on Jethro's back and grabs his arms, folding them behind him. Jethro is handcuffed, but his mouth is still going:

"Bind Annie to me.
"Bind Annie only to me, Jethro.
"Spirit of the Dead."

Police Officer Cole begins to read Jethro his rights while Officer Corey grabs Jethro's legs and begins to hoist him up.

Both officers carry Jethro to the patrol car. The dolls, the strands of Annie's hair, and the sock fall into the hole that was being dug by Jethro during the scuffle.

FADE TO CUMBERLAND COUNTY POLICE DEPARTMENT

JETHRO: "What about my phone call? Don't I get a phone call?"

DUTY OFFICER JESSE: "You'll get your phone call soon. Calm down, buddy."

JETHRO: "I want my freaking phone call!"

DUTY OFFICER JESSE: "From what hole did you pick this guy up, Cole?"

POLICE OFFICER COLE: "Inside of Claremont cemetery. He was in the middle of chanting some kind of spell. Had a couple of dolls in his hand."

DUTY OFFICER JESSE: "You're kidding me."

POLICE OFFICER COLE: "I kid you not. I don't make up shit like this."

DUTY OFFICER JESSE: "You sure know how to pick 'em."

POLICE OFFICER COLE: "That's for sure."

DUTY OFFICER JESSE: "Can you do me a favor and take him downstairs so he can make his call? Otherwise he'll drive me nuts. I'll have to give him an attitude adjustment."

POLICE OFFICER COLE: "No problem. Okay, Mr. Orrick, let's take a walk. You have ten minutes to make your call. I hope you have a credit card number."

Jethro is too ashamed and embarrassed to call any of his army buddies. He calls the only one who will believe his foolish but harmless intentions. Of all the phone numbers he remembers, he calls the phone number of Psychic Cindy.

PSYCHIC CINDY: "Hello?"

JETHRO: "Cindy? Did I call at a bad time?"

PSYCHIC CINDY: "No, it's never a bad time. How are you?"

JETHRO: "Well, that's kind of what I wanted to talk about."

PSYCHIC CINDY: "Why? What happened?"

JETHRO: "I'm kind of in a jam. I'm incarcerated at Cumberland County jail in North Carolina."

PSYCHIC CINDY: "What the hell did you do?"

JETHRO: "It's kind of a long story."

PSYCHIC CINDY: "Well, Jethro, I have time and right now it looks like you have plenty of time."

JETHRO: "I picked up a book of spells. I was following the chapter from Santeria darkness."

PSYCHIC CINDY: "What? You bought that book? You used the binding spell? Then that's why you're in jail. The cemetery will always bury you, my love."

JETHRO: "I was arrested for trespassing at a local cemetery."

PSYCHIC CINDY: "People don't believe me. You can't make this shit up."

JETHRO: "My bail is $1,850.00."

PSYCHIC CINDY: "That's a bit high for trespassing."

JETHRO: "This is North Carolina. They make up their own prices."

PSYCHIC CINDY: "Jethro, I can't bail you out, if that's what you're thinking."

JETHRO: "Cindy, please. I'll pay you back. You know I'm good for it. No one else will even bother with me. You're the only one I can count on."

PSYCHIC CINDY: "On top of that, I'll have to drive to North Carolina; this is a joke, right? Maybe this is a dream. I must have fallen asleep, right? My pet dog is wiggling my toes."

JETHRO: "I have to get out of here, Cindy. I have a cell mate, and he's starting to look at me funny. He has this horny look on his face. I think he wants to make me his bitch. Please!"

PSYCHIC CINDY: "I'm including the cost of gas and tolls with the bail. I'm including any motel stay as well."

JETHRO: "Whatever it takes, I'll pay you back."

PSYCHIC CINDY: "It's going to take me a couple of hours to get ready."

JETHRO: "Cindy, you're the best."

Cindy gets off the phone with Jethro and is screaming at the top of her lungs in Spanish: *"Puneta, no me joder, maricon, to me esta jodiendo."* She starts her trip to North Carolina. Eighteen hours later Jethro is a free man and headed home. He wants no part of Cumberland County. Exhausted from the trip, Cindy has a brief stay at a local motel. The following day she heads back home.

Meanwhile back at the graveyard:

The graveyard caretaker, Igor, refills the hole left by Jethro's brief ceremony. The dolls are buried along with the strand of Annie's hair and Jethro's sock. Unknown to Jethro, the burying of these items completes the spell.

FROM THE MIND OF ANNIE

I decided that I needed to see for myself who this "Betty" woman is. Jethro always told me when he was leaving that he was coming back in three weeks. That meant he was going home, down South.

Five days after he left, I headed down South. I wanted to give him enough time to arrive and get comfortable with his wife. I knew his habits, and usually he stays around for a while once he got there. I wanted to make sure that he was there when I arrived. I was going to confront him and expose more to his wife. When I arrived at his home, it was still light outside. I parked away from the house and observed that the blinds were open wide and heard music playing. My arm was bothering me from the long trip. I closed my eyes to relax before I exited the car. Quietly I approached the walkway and came up to the front door. I pressed the doorbell. After a few seconds I heard:

JETHRO: "Can you get that, honey?"

The door opens.

UNKNOWN WHITE WOMAN: "Hi, can I help you?"

ANNIE: "Who are you?"

UNKNOWN WHITE WOMAN: "I'm Betty, Jethro's wife."

Annie's left hand is hidden behind her. She moves her hand slowly into her back pocket, where a small knife is hidden.

ANNIE: "Yeah, well, I'm Annie, Jethro's girlfriend. This is for you, bitch!!"

Annie takes out the knife and starts to swing her left arm toward Betty. She feels her left arm locking up and hurting and realizes that she's dreaming. She is still in the car. Her head is spinning from the effect of the Vicodin. Annie realizes she must have fallen asleep from the effect of the medication she's on.

As she clears her head, she glances at the house. The music is still playing, but now she hears Jethro talking loud with a woman. It's dark out, and she still feels a little groggy. She gets out of the car and heads up the walkway to the front door of the house.

She presses the doorbell, and like déjà vu, the scene is played out again.

JETHRO: "Can you get that, honey?"

The door opens; a voluptuous-looking black woman stands at the entrance. She has a horrified look on her face as she sees Annie.

UNKNOWN BLACK WOMAN: "You're Annie, right? I recognize you from the e-mail photos. What are you doing here?"

Annie is puzzled by the woman's remark.

ANNIE: "Who are you?"

UNKNOWN BLACK WOMAN: "I'm Betty. I'm Jethro's wife!"

Coney Island

Sometimes when we want to be alone, we park the truck under the boardwalk at Coney Island. Carl, sitting in the driver's seat, pushes the seat back and lays there while I explore his muscular body with my hands and start to kiss him passionately. I unzip his pants, pull them down halfway. His fully erect penis pops out, nearly hitting me in the face. I grab his sex organ with my mouth and swallow deeply 'til it hits the back of my throat. I feel his penis growing as Carl holds on to the back of my head, stroking my hair....

FADE TO FULL STORY

My name is Vanessa. I'm married to my husband, Vinnie, for over twenty-seven years. I work as an office manager for the Transit Authority. My husband, Vinnie, is a dry cleaner. Vinnie is a very quiet man, very family-oriented, but does not have that closeness with the children that some parents have. We have three boys, ages twelve, sixteen, and nineteen.

One day while I was out for lunch on Broadway, I dropped my napkin. When I went down to pick it up, my head almost bumped into another head with the most adorable green eyes I've ever seen. Leaning over to pick up my napkin was this six-foot-tall man who looked more like a Viking God.

As he offers me his own napkin, I could see his huge arms shiny with sweat pouring down causing my own sweat glands to ignite with excitement.

Suddenly everyone around me disappears. I know people are talking, but I can't hear them. All I could see and fantasize about at that moment was this Viking-size man taking me by force.

It's been two years, and Carl and I are still together. Carl has tried to leave his wife, but says he cannot leave his children behind. He has two daughters, age twenty one and eighteen. I would never ask him to leave, but I still want to be with him at all times. I can't imagine why any woman in her right mind would turn Carl down.

Everything was going along fine with Carl. It was my home life that was starting to be affected. I started to develop what I called Carl-vision. Every time I look at my husband, Vinnie, I see Carl instead. On top of that, I began to imagine Carl with other women. This was beginning to become a problem. How could I be jealous of a man I was seeing behind my husband's back? One way or another, Carl was going to belong to me and no one else.

VANESSA SEEKS THE HELP AND ADVICE
OF MRS. MARTINEZ ON MATTERS OF THE HEART

Mrs. Martinez is a gypsy woman new to the area. Unknown to many of her clients, she has a 50/50 record of success. Vanessa hears that Mrs. Martinez does the practice of Santeria. Mrs. Martinez agrees to see Vanessa and asks her to come to her place. Vanessa walks up the driveway to a house with a black wrought-iron fenced-in area. Vanessa unlatches the fence and comes up to the front door. She rings the doorbell twice, and ten seconds later the door swings open.

VANESSA: "Mrs. Martinez!"

MRS. MARTINEZ: "Yes, hello. You must be Vanessa. So happy to meet you."

Vanessa looks at Mrs. Martinez like a child looks at a dentist about to pull his teeth.

MRS. MARTINEZ: "Come right in, dear, I won't bite you. No problem with the directions, I hope."

VANESSA: "Not at all."

MRS. MARTINEZ: "I know how difficult it is to seek help. Things can't change unless you make it happen. I can make it happen your way. I guarantee it."

VANESSA: "You guarantee it?"

MRS. MARTINEZ: "Yes, I do. How many psychics do you know give you a guarantee?"

VANESSA: "You're the first one."

MRS. MARTINEZ: "There you go. Let me show you what I can do for you. You're here because you seek to torment the man you love. This man avoids you, no?"

VANESSA: "How do you know this?"

MRS. MARTINEZ: "When I spoke to you over the phone, I read your despair. I could feel your cry for help. I said to myself, I can help this woman and bring back her true love."

VANESSA: "You can?"

MRS. MARTINEZ: "Yes, I can. You must follow specific instructions. Only the In Tranquil Spirit must be called upon to lure out your love."

VANESSA: "Did you say the In Tranquil Spirit?"

MRS. MARTINEZ: "Yes, the In Tranquil Spirit. This is a very powerful spirit. This spirit is called upon by a spell. This spell is very expensive."

VANESSA: "How expensive is this spell?"

MRS. MARTINEZ: "This one will cost you five hundred dollars."

VANESSA: "It costs five hundred dollars for a spell?"

MRS. MARTINEZ: "That's why I guarantee it. It will take you where you want to go. It will give you what you want. No questions asked."

VANESSA: "How fast is this going to happen?"

MRS. MARTINEZ: "Just a matter of days."

Vanessa is so desperate, she asks to be excused and returns half an hour later with the money. Vanessa is skeptical at first, but also terrified of what Mrs. Martinez could do.

VANESSA: "Can we begin this process now, Mrs. Martinez?"

MRS. MARTINEZ: "We absolutely can. These are my instructions to you: First you must place a picture of your lover in a jar filled with rose petals. Keep this jar in your closet. I will prepare a special candle for you. This candle is red and must be kept in a brown paper bag. The candle must be kept in the darkness until it grants you your wish. You must talk to it."

VANESSA: "What do I have to say to it?"

MRS. MARTINEZ: "You will tell it that it will only get lit when it grants you your wish. Your wish is as follows:

'Hear me, In Tranquil Spirit, spirit that wanders hell for all eternity
I want you to grab my lover's mind and not let him rest until
He thinks only of me, until he only smells me, sees and only hears me
Do not let him rest until he comes defeated to me
When he touches anything, make him feel that he is touching me.
Let him feel these things until he returns to me.

Do not give him peace until he stumbles and falls.
Allow him to look stupid and foolish to all.
That no one should ever love him but me,
That until you, In Tranquil Spirit, grant me these wishes, I
Will keep you in this brown bag at the bottom of this dark closet starving
    for light
I will only light you to free you from the grips of hell, when
My lover is by my side. When my lover is a slave for
My love and no one else's love, then you will be free.'"

Vanessa is terrified by her session with Mrs. Martinez. It takes her a while to get up the nerve to admit she has been swindled during a moment of desperation. Through her mingling with her associates, she hears about a popular psychic named Psychic Cindy. She finally makes an appointment to see Psychic Cindy.

OFFICE OF PSYCHIC CINDY,
CLIENT VANESSA SANCHEZ'S FIRST SESSION

Vanessa walks into the office of Psychic Cindy.

PSYCHIC CINDY: "Hi, I'm Cindy. How are you?"

VANESSA: "Hi, my name is Vanessa Sanchez, but people call me Nessa."

PSYCHIC CINDY: "Fine, Nessa, that's what I'll call you. On the phone, you mentioned some bad experience you had."

VANESSA: "Yes, I'm not very experienced seeing psychics. I've lost a considerable amount of money because of my ignorance."

PSYCHIC CINDY: "Well, I'm sorry you had a bad experience. I'm going to describe some events and things that I feel and see. All you have to do is listen to my reading. I hope to make your reading experience a pleasant one. I strive for accurate readings."

VANESSA: "I was a little bit apprehensive when I first came in. I'm feeling better now."

As the morning goes by, Vanessa begins to feel more comfortable about being read. When Vanessa responds to her reading, Cindy listens and absorbs everything she hears. Cindy continues with the reading and describes what she feels and sees to Vanessa.

The more Vanessa relaxes, the more she begins to let her body language reveal her persona. Because of her years of experience with clients, Cindy knows and understands how to read body language. Vanessa stands about 5 feet 4 inches, with a more-to-love type body and short blonde hair. She has green eyes and a dreamy, sexy look. The thing about Vanessa is that the more she tries to hide her natural sex appeal, the more it comes out. Cindy's reading brings out that Vanessa is a bit of a flirt when it comes to men.

Psychic Cindy knows there is more to Vanessa than just being an ordinary wife. This was her first reading, and Vanessa was doing well and feeling good about the reading. The reading would end with Vanessa feeling good about herself and wanting to return for another session. That was always a big plus.

FROM THE MIND OF VANESSA

Carl and I spend as much time together as we can. Our favorite place is under the boardwalk at Coney Island. After a ten-minute walk, we head back to sit in his truck. Carl always likes to play with my hair. Carl pushes the driver's seat back and lies there while I massage him to ecstasy. I always perform oral on Carl, and it has become a welcome routine for him.

One day something happens while we have sex under the boardwalk. A man is standing in front of the truck just watching. Carl, startled, jumps up, pushes me to the next seat, pulls his pants up, and jumps out of the truck. Carl pulls at the guy's jacket .The guy reacts by putting his hands up and says,

ROBERT: "What do you expect? She is beautiful! If it's all right with you, I would like some of that action."

CARL: "You know, you scared the crap out of me!"

ROBERT: "Sorry. Didn't mean to, but your lady is hot. I don't know if you're into a threesome."

CARL: "It depends on the moment."

ROBERT: "It's always a passion of mine to watch. How long have you been coming here?"

CARL: "I've been coming here about two weeks. But it's a pretty isolated place. I like coming here because of the risk."

ROBERT: "What do you mean?"

CARL: "There's an excitement that comes along with getting caught or busted."

ROBERT: "I can understand that. I like to look, and it's more exciting to think someone will catch me."

CARL: "Exactly."

ROBERT: "What's your name?"

CARL: "Sorry, my name is Carl. My girl is Vanessa."

ROBERT: "Hi, Carl, my name is Robert. Carl, you think I can have some of this action now?"

CARL: "Wait. Let me tell my lady what the deal is."

FROM THE MIND OF VANESSA

As I watch from inside the truck, I see Carl's face change from anger to excitement. Carl comes in and says, "Hey, baby, I have an idea. My new friend Robert would like to sit next to us in the passenger seat. He wants you in the middle."

With Carl and Robert sitting in the truck, Robert takes the captain's seat and leans it back. I know this is what Carl wants, so I remove Robert's pants and give him pleasure. I could see that this seems to excite my lover, Carl. More than anything I want to keep him happy, so I continue to give pleasure to Robert. Carl removes my clothes and positions me between his legs, where he enters me repeatedly. Carl loves doing it under the boardwalk. He's like a boy with a brand-new toy. Robert likes the idea of playing the bystander who gets some action, and I just like pleasing Carl no matter what it takes. This was our twisted ritual every Thursday for six months.

I have been on anti-depression medicine for several years now. My doctor has diagnosed me as having a split personality. This secret I have kept for years. At times I can be very sweet, but I can also be sociopathic .At one time I was a home health aide and took care of an elderly lady named Jane. This is where my other personality got the best of me.

I don't know what came over me. I felt the need to have Jane's husband. I knew it was wrong, but I couldn't help myself. I always get what I want, and I was going to have Jane's husband.

SCENE AT THE HOME OF JANE STROCKTON

JOHN STROCKTON: "How long did the doctor say Jane will be at the clinic?"

VANESSA: "I have to go pick her up at 1 p.m. The doctor said the procedure will have her a bit weak when she comes home. Must be hard on you."

JOHN: "Yes, it is. I love her dearly. I hate to see her this way."

VANESSA: "You know, John, maybe I can help you."

JOHN: "You've been helpful already."

VANESSA: "No, I don't mean with the housework. I mean you can lean on me for advice or comfort. I don't mind."

JOHN: "Thank you, Vanessa. Don't know what we would do without you."

VANESSA: "I find you a very honest and passionate man. Your wife is very lucky."

JOHN: "You're making me self-conscious now. You're just teasing me."

I could see that John was a bit startled while I flirted with him; there was a part of him that wanted to say no. That part was beginning to weaken the more I enticed him with my sexual charms. As I approached him and began massaging his shoulders, I could sense him getting weaker by the minute.

JOHN: "That feels so good, Vanessa. You're going to get me in trouble with Jane."

VANESSA: "You're uptight. Don't you want to feel better? Tell you what…It just has to be our little secret. Everyone has a little secret, right, John?"

The aroma of my perfume must have brought out the beast in John. He grabbed my leg and fondled the back of my thigh. That was enough to get me going. I leaned over to kiss him and grabbed his crotch. He was as hard as a diamond. There was no stopping our exploration of each other's bodies. Ten minutes later I was in his bed and he was inside me. I could feel the tension he had been holding for two years since his wife stopped making love to him because of her illness.

I began an affair with Jane's husband that lasted three years. Two of those years I was still married to my husband, Vinnie. When the affair with John ended, I didn't realize that I was pregnant.

My husband assumed that the baby was his. Why would he ever suspect that he is not the biological father to our baby?

Jane finds out about the affair and decides to get revenge. Jane feels betrayed. How could this woman look at her in the face every day, nurse her back to health, yet at the same time sleep with her husband? She finds out when Vanessa gets out of work and plans her move. Jane puts a "NOT WORKING" sign on the elevator outside of Vanessa's office. She waits inside the stairwell. Vanessa walks out and sees the sign. She opens the door and heads for the stairs. Vanessa feels strange, as if someone is behind her, and pauses to turn around.

VANESSA: "Jane, you scared the sh*t out of me! What are you doing here?"

Jane looks into Vanessa's eyes with bad intentions. Vanessa can see that Jane knows about her and John.

VANESSA: "I'm sorry, Jane. I didn't mean to hurt you. Couldn't help myself."

JANE: "Yeah, well, you did hurt me. You didn't mean to have my husband's penis inside you either?"

VANESSA: "Jane, I really don't want to talk about this."

JANE: "You self-righteous bitch! You f*ck my husband and you don't wanna talk about it? John wants to leave me now, you f*cking slut. You're carrying my baby, bitch! That's supposed to be my baby. That's my f*cking baby!"

VANESSA: "You know what? I can see where this is headed, so I'm out of here."

Vanessa refuses to get upset. She turns her back on Jane to head down the stairs. This infuriates Jane.

JANE: "Go ahead; turn your back on me. It's my turn to hurt you, bitch!"

Jane pushes Vanessa. Vanessa is surprised and falls all the way to the bottom landing. Jane walks down, looks at Vanessa, and walks by her unconscious body. She spits in her face and continues to head outside the building as if nothing has happened.

Vanessa loses the baby because of the fall. Jane is picked up later and charged with manslaughter and aggravated assault. Jane was found wandering half-naked and taken to Creedmoor State Mental Hospital. Because of the miscarriage, Vinnie finds out about the affair. He is unsure how to handle this. His emotions run high, but he holds everything inside without voicing his hurt.

Vinnie changes his demeanor and now has a huge chip on his shoulder. His cold attitude is evident when he looks at anyone. Like a person without sleep, his eyes have deep circles around them. Vinnie starts to realize that his middle son is getting like him. His middle son is getting further away from society and always angry at everything. The middle son grows resentment toward his older brother because of the closeness between the older brother and mother.

Meanwhile Vanessa is continuing life with Carl as the affair continues in full swing. She doesn't realize her home is falling apart. Vanessa is very unhappy because she doesn't know how to say goodbye to her life with Vinnie.

One day the boys are all fighting over things that boys typically fight over. The father encourages the middle son to beat on the younger one. The older brother steps in to defend the younger boy. He hits the father instead. He knows the father is wrong and tells Vanessa about it.

FADE TO THE OFFICE OF PSYCHIC CINDY

With tears in their eyes and at their breaking point, clients sometimes show up with Cindy's favorite snacks.

A CONVERSATION OVER CINDY'S FAVORITE,
GLAZED DUNKIN' DONUTS AND FRENCH VANILLA COFFEE

PSYCHIC CINDY: "You know, Vanessa, you can't have your cake and eat it, too. From everything that you've told me, it seems that you're not ready to let go of your lifestyle."

VANESSA: "I keep trying, but somehow I become weak. I especially become weak when it comes to Carl. There's just something about that man. He drains any morals out of me."

PSYCHIC CINDY: "Yes, but you also became weak with someone else's husband, Vanessa."

VANESSA: "You mean John?"

PSYCHIC CINDY: "Yes, Vanessa, I mean John and Robert in the truck? Hello? Well, Vanessa, this is something that only you can fix. I sense that there is some kind of addiction here."

VANESSA: "You saying I have an addiction?"

PSYCHIC CINDY: "Yes, addiction."

VANESSA: "You mean, like drugs?"

Vanessa becomes self-conscious and instantly wipes away imaginary coke trails from her nostrils.

VANESSA: "I don't do anything like that."

PSYCHIC CINDY: "No, Vanessa, I'm not talking about that kind of addiction. Your addiction is of a sexual nature. Unless you get it under control, it will continue to break down your family. Look what happened to you. Do you really want to continue down this road?"

VANESSA: "But if I do have an addiction, how do I get rid of it?"

PSYCHIC CINDY: "It's treated like any other addiction, one day at a time. First step you need to do is admit to it."

VANESSA: "Admit to it?"

PSYCHIC CINDY: "Yes. You're addicted to sex. Well?"

VANESSA: "Yes, I suppose you're right."

PSYCHIC CINDY: "Now that wasn't too hard, was it? That's a beginning, Vanessa. That's the first step, Vanessa. One step at a time."

VANESSA: "Where do I go from here, Cindy?"

PSYCHIC CINDY: "Take care of your family. Your family comes first. Everything else after. Always ask yourself, if you have a question, 'How's this going to affect my family?' If you need to ask me anything, I'm here for you. If you want a reading, don't hesitate to call me. I want to hear from you. Don't forget, I'm here for you."

INSIDE THE MIND OF VANESSA
WHEN SHE'S BACK HOME BY HERSELF

I love you today, Psychic Cindy, but tomorrow I will hate you. I want to spit on you at times, then I also need to have you near me when my fears come back to haunt me. Many times I bounce off my animosity toward you. I love your accuracy when you read me. I can hate you for it as well. I cuss you when you remove my shields. I struggle to understand my actions and feelings. You are always willing to ride along with me, no matter what.

What am I going to do about Carl?

Vanessa is horrified about what happened. She thought the boys would resent her if she left. She realized its best if the boys are away from their father at this time. Vanessa looks for an apartment in New Jersey and moves the boys out.

Vanessa has an extremely close relationship with her sons. Her sons know everything about Carl. The children have helped her to find an apartment in the next two boroughs so Carl and she could have a place to call home. This is a place that will be filled with our love. It started out that way, now Vanessa made this a cozy home to come to, embraced with lots of warmth. One year later at the boys' New Jersey apartment, there's a knock on the door.

VANESSA: "Carl, what are you doing here?"

CARL: "Hi, Vanessa, can I stay with you and the boys?"

The Trucker

My name is Lisa. I am forty years old, five feet seven inches, slim, with reddish-color hair, medium length. I've been a dentist for the past six years. I've had many relationships, including some with married men.

My parents are from and still live in Virginia. They pray to God that I would find the right man and finally settle down. My biological clock is ticking away, and I feel that I may not find the husband that I seek or the children that I see in my future. I light candles and pray to God every day for the right man to come along. I admit that I'm getting desperate as time goes by. I maintain that the best way to keep a man is to take a special interest in his hobbies. This interest includes his occupation as well. Once a week I have been seeing a psychic for the past four years. My advisor is known as Psychic Cindy. Cindy has a unique way of making me feel comfortable enough to reveal my inner thoughts and feelings. She also has an incredible memory for things that I've told her over the years.

I meet a lot of men on a daily basis, and as psychic Cindy has warned me I am all over the place sleeping with every Tom, Dick & Harry. They say in my desperation for the right one I find myself being abused emotionally and mentally for sex, but at the end of the day it's the scariest thing; I don't care! Who is sicker, the men I find or me? During one of my sessions with Cindy, I revealed that seven months ago I joined a popular online dating service and have been on a few dates. The dating service was not all it was cracked up to be. It did not lead to the type of man I was looking for.

George is a man I have dated on and off for ten years. He is in his forties and wears a hairpiece. George is a writer. I've had two abortions, yet I still live and breathe for this man, God only knows why. I still pray to God that one day he will marry me. He is the type of man who abuses you verbally and emotionally. It's always my fault...I misunderstand...I don't get things right. Gee, I'm starting to wonder, is it really me? I have to ask myself what is wrong with me. Why do I want to hold on to this man?

George agrees after multiple discussions to father a child with me but through fertility, and then he surprises me by wanting me to sign a document relieving him of all child support. Gee, why I am not surprised? But I do it anyway.

He likes the idea that I work for Changes, a strip club. He also likes to have sex on his office desk. That is his kinky side. The excitement of having sex on his desk was like a ritual for him. On the floor at Changes, his lust for me was out of control. The security team always seems to appear out of nowhere when he walks into the club. Security knew how out of control he got.

They could somehow sense his sexual hunger. This lust for me would fade when I later quit the club. George was like every other guy walking into a strip club. The excitement for him was always about having sex with a stripper. George has multiple women in his life. He is very successful. He thinks I stalk him every chance I get. He believes in his mind that I am some kind of psycho. The reason for this is because I treat him like my king. I bring him nice shirts and pants to wear. I always go out of my way for him. Call to see if he is okay, bring him lunch, walk and feed his yorkie.

Sometimes, I would show up at his job, close the door to his office, and just spread myself. He was always hungry, and for this I was labeled a stalker. During my ten years of dating George, I met another man named Peter. I was really attracted to him, and he looked a lot like George. It may sound rather strange, but it's true. I wonder if other women look for guys who look like their past lovers.

This was true in the beginning when I met Peter. As time went by, I began to see and appreciate Peter's unique qualities. To my surprise, my memories of George would become history. Peter was my new man.

My Psychic calls Peter "Mr. Wonderful."

I told her that she gave him the right name. He comes on very sweet—too sweet at times, but after a while you have to wonder: Is there really such a man who truly is Mr. Wonderful? It begins to eat at you. She looked at me and gave me an "I don't want to know" smile. Peter operates a trucking business and smuggles drugs into the state while making his deliveries. He makes a lot of money and always buys me expensive gifts

Peter is married. He has a daughter and an older daughter from a previous marriage. He convinces me to give up my night job at Changes. I would leave at times and then go back when I was feeling lonely or bored, at times not realizing I have this crave for attention. He has made numerous promises to me about giving me a better life and children; however now things are starting to turn around in a not so good way. Peter is starting to call me only when he wants to fulfill his fantasies. It's been several months now that Peter and I are together. He has stopped mentioning having a family; am I being naive or just plain DUMB! My friends are telling me so I decided to seek the services of a fertility clinic. I visited the fertility clinic several times before. More than anything else I wanted a baby in my life, I was willing and ready to have this baby with Peter but how long will I have to wait? The first time I had sex with Peter I knew it was going to be great! It's a feeling you can't explain. Peter has a way of embracing me that makes me feel excited right away. I take my hand and reach between my legs. I wet my fingers and place them on Peter's lips. I love the way Peter reacts to this. The aroma always drove him to erection heaven. Peter reacts by grabbing my leg and swinging it over his shoulder. He places his head between my legs. I locked my legs around his neck. His mouth meets my vagina and I enter a state of euphoria, where time stands still. I don't know how many orgasms I had, but Peter took me to the point of no return. I could never look at trucks the same way again without thinking of my guy Peter.

Thomas is a man I met from the dating service. Thomas is a pilot, has lots of money. He's a real heartthrob and has a powerful job. The third time we dated, there was excitement in the air. We knew this was the night we would have sex. I could sense the nervousness in Thomas and his tense movements. After dinner we walked together and talked for a while before deciding to go to his place. When we reached his place, Thomas offered me a drink to set the mood. I was already wet and frustrated in anticipation. Thomas reached over to me and smelled my hair. He looked into my eyes and forced his tongue into my mouth. It was too soon and he was a bit rough. As wet as I was at that point, I didn't care.

I reached down and squeezed his penis, which was already hard. I enjoyed the power I had at that moment. I could ask him for anything as long as I held on and stroked him the right way. He peeled his clothes off and I removed my blouse and bra. He reached over and grabbed my panties and ripped them off. He pushed me back onto the bed, grabbed my waist, and began to explore my mouth with his tongue. Sliding his hand between my legs, he worked his middle finger inside and violated me to ecstasy.

LISA: "I only want you to violate me, Tom. Tom, only you know how to do me, baby."

THOMAS: "Like this, baby?"

LISA: "No, not like that. You need to use more than one finger. Okay, yeah, that's the way. I like that, baby. Just like that. Deeper. Deeper, baby. Now you got it. Awwwwwww."

THOMAS: "Shit f*ck."

LISA: "Talk dirty to me, baby. Talk dirty to me."

I reached over to grab his erection, but now it was soft, spongy, and lifeless. I could see by the look in his face that he was in trouble. I needed to feel him inside me, but his erection was gone. He apologized for the moment, and revealed that he had erectile dysfunction. He took Viagra to enhance his conquest. Thomas's problem appears to be more psychological than physical. The pill was not working.

Thomas apologized like a fifteen-year-old just experiencing sex for the first time. At that moment he looked vulnerable. I grabbed him and held him closer to me. We laid there in each other's arms and eventually sleep took us over. I knew that this awkward moment would pass and was happy just being there with him.

He dropped a bomb on me one day when he revealed that he was seeing his ex-girlfriend from his past who suddenly surfaced out of nowhere. He was honest in telling me that he had strong desires to continue this friendship from the past. I was crushed by this rejection. At that moment I felt nothing but hatred for the man.

I said to myself, "Why is this happening to me?" I blame myself for being too fat and not being attractive enough. I hated him and myself. I even blamed myself for not being sexy enough to keep him aroused.

A few months later, out of nowhere, I got a call from Thomas. He wanted to see me. I felt a bit of desperation and an apologetic tone in his voice. When I spoke with him, he told me that he made a mistake. It turned out that his ex-girlfriend was just using him for his money and had no intentions of entering into a long-term relationship. I have to admit that at this point the devil in me took over. I had absolutely no sympathy for the man.

Of course deep down inside, I was happy to hear this. I would never show him this emotion. Would I take him back right away? Or would I make him sweat it out for a while? I told him that I had to think about where I wanted to go with him. I even lied to him and told him that I had met another man and needed to see where I was going with him.

I did not want to close the door to Thomas, just wanted to get even and make him sweat a little, so I agreed to meet up with him the following week for a date. I told Thomas that I would call him to secure the date. This time it was my turn to be in control, and I wanted to make him sweat a little. Who was I kidding? I really wanted to see him. I wanted to grab him and rip off his clothes. I desired to make passionate love to him. How can any woman resist him, I wonder?

I still had strong feelings for Thomas, and it was him that I wanted to be with most of all. Now I know I have to be rid of Peter. I called Peter and told him that I needed to talk to him about our relationship. I would meet with him and break the news to him gently. The first mistake I made was meeting Peter. The second mistake I made was meeting him in a motel.

My meeting with Peter didn't exactly go the way I expected. What should have been a fifteen-minute goodbye turned into an all-nighter. Peter convinced me that it would be our final night, and I agreed to it. Once again, I was a slave to his sexual prowess. Our breakup sex was good, but this would be the last time I saw Peter.

LISA: "You're not playing fair, Peter."

PETER: "Why, don't you like what I'm doing?"

LISA: "It's just that you know how weak I get when you touch me."

PETER: "Like this?"

LISA: "Oh, Peter, what am I going to do with you? Stop. Please stop."

PETER: "Okay, I'll stop."

LISA: "No, don't stop now, fool, I'm coming!"

Peter pressed up against me and the wall, where I could feel his erection growing between my legs. He reached behind my thigh and gently squeezed my buttocks, igniting sexual sensation throughout my body. Once again I found myself lying down on the bed and opening my flower to allow Peter in to savor the ovule.

Another man I dated was Brian, an attorney. He is five feet, two inches, reddish-color hair, owned his own construction, is now retired and is building a house in New Rochelle. I wanted to scream when I first saw him. He was a lot shorter than I had imagined. Tall men are very seductive to me. I get weak in my knees when I'm near them. What he lacked in height, he made up for in the bedroom.

The sex was good, but for some reason I kept calling out other guys' names instead of his during our most intimate moments. Calling out some other guy's name in the heat of passion drove him absolutely mad. I didn't blame him for feeling this way, but I just couldn't help myself. It was Thomas's name that I screamed out the most. Brian kept yelling, "Fu*k Thomas! I'm not f**king Thomas! Who the hell is Thomas?"

Of all the men I dated, Thomas made me feel very secure. I decided to end all dating and surrender to his love. During one of my sessions with my therapist, Psychic Cindy revealed to me that I am in deep trouble in my search for a husband. Well, she was right. I am five weeks' pregnant. During routine blood work, the doctor stated the blood test confirmed that I am pregnant!

AT THE OFFICE OF PSYCHIC CINDY

LISA: "Cindy, I wanted you to be the first to know."

PSYCHIC CINDY: "Know what?"

LISA: "I went to the doctor for blood work. I'm pregnant!"

Psychic Cindy looks on in horror, lights a cigarette, and asks with a cynical laugh:

PSYCHIC CINDY: "Who's the father? Is it Thomas? Peter? The fertility clinic?"

CHAPTER TWO
BADA-BING BADA-BOOM

I t was 4 a.m. I put the "Be Right Back" sign up on the door. Delores reaches over, unbuckles my pants, and slides them and my jockeys off my hips. I grab her from her hips and lift her onto the counter. As I position her between my legs, the silverware, cups, and saucers go flying off, crashing to the floor. I can feel her sink her nails into my back with anticipation. She wants me in the worst way, and I am not about to let this moment pass, no matter what. I knew she was begging for it and I was going to give it to her. She finds my throbbing penis and rides me like she's being paid. The remaining dishes that are on the counter shake in synchronized motion with every pelvic thrust.

This was a great way to baptize my diner, and I felt it was good luck. More than anything, I knew that Delores came to see me, wanted me, and only I could satisfy her desires.

FADE TO RAYMOND'S STORY

My name is Raymond. I am six feet tall, forty-nine years old, but I look more like thirty-four. For many years my dad worked as a cook struggling to put food on the table. My mom worked as a seamstress in a Bronx factory on Park Avenue. All I could dream about was one day owning my own restaurant, so I wouldn't have to struggle like my father did. It was more important for me to spend time with my father.

My attempt to speed up my goals was unsuccessful. I tried to get into the drug business to make some fast money. Fast money in the drug trade is always met with high risk. One day I wound up getting pinched and had to do some time. This was the same time that my dad's drinking caught up to him. He became ill and had to stay in the hospital. More than anyone, my mom was deeply affected by this. She and my dad have been together for more than thirty years.

It was time for me to make my move. Like a light bulb turning on in my head, it was then that I decided to move out and get a place of my own.

I needed to show my dad that I understood life and knew how to take care of business. I didn't want to disappoint my mom, either. I still had some money that I stashed away from my drug business. I found a small place on Webster Avenue near the Fordham Road section of the Bronx. This would be my pride and joy. I named the restaurant Papi's Café.

Life had been good to me. I had a restaurant in my name; it was so successful I decided to open another one in Manhattan named Chorizo. The restaurant business gave me the opportunity to meet lots of women. It was my fiftieth birthday and I started the day off fighting with my girlfriend, Blanca. I lost track of how many times I broke up and made up with her. It was the price you paid for going with someone a lot younger than you. It was easy to attract younger women when you are as successful as I am. I wouldn't have it any other way, I like them young. On top of that, I was in the prime of my life. I decided to stay at the restaurant all day, to keep my mind off Blanca.

SOMEWHERE IN THE BACK OFFICE OF RESTAURANT CHORIZO

RAFAEL: "I took care of the delivery problem for you."

RAYMOND: "Remember, I don't want any traces to my restaurant Chorizo or to me."

RAFAEL: "What's to stop him from getting supplies from another house?"

RAYMOND: "You. I want you to make it hard for him. Discourage him."

RAFAEL: "What if he gets suspicious, Raymond?"

RAYMOND: "I'll worry about that."

RAFAEL: "But, Raymond, he's just a small fry. Why worry about this guy?"

RAYMOND: "He's a small fry today. Tomorrow I may have to work for this guy. Find out who his other suppliers are. I guarantee they're not going to do business with him."

RAFAEL: "How many suppliers, Raymond?"

RAYMOND: "All of them. Every stinking supplier, no matter how small. Find out who supplies him the ingredients. I don't give a f*#k what they sell him. Make sure it doesn't get to his restaurant."

RAFAEL: "You'll put him out of business before he even gets started."

RAYMOND: "Exactly. That's the idea."

RAYMOND: "Here, this is for the other job."

Raymond hands him a sealed bulky brown envelope.

RAYMOND: "You do good work, Raymond's going to take care of you. You know, that motherf*cker used to work for me."

RAFAEL: "No way!"

RAYMOND: "Now he's trying to steal some of my customers. If this doesn't work, then I'll have to cancel his contract. If you know what I mean."

RAFAEL: "Whatever needs to be done, Raymond. I'm with you, boss, all the way."

Raymond gives Rafael a bear hug to cement their understanding. He is careful to use code words in the event that he is being recorded. Raymond trusts no one. He would just as easily get rid of Rafael in the blink of an eye as he would put on another pair of socks. Raymond always talks to his boys alone. This is an easy way to find a snitch. He never gives one job to two people. If one of his guys gets pinched, he only knows his job, not the other guy's business.

Raymond is the pickiest person when it comes to choosing his personnel. When it comes to hiring any women, he has to see them personally as part of the hiring process. Raymond has been known to fire some of the women because they put on too much weight or have self-esteem issues. A real sleazy guy, it doesn't take much to get Raymond excited.

Raymond interviews Jessica for a waiter position at his restaurant Chorizo. Unknown to Raymond, Jessica wants the job to seduce Raymond. She likes to control powerful men and their money. During the interview she wears a white button-down blouse. Her blouse is opened to reveal her cleavage. She also has on a short blue miniskirt and matching high heel pumps.

Jessica greets Raymond at the door. Raymond asks her to take a seat in front of him. She sits and crosses her legs as Raymond starts the interview process. Raymond grabs his notepad and a chair and sits about six feet in front of her.

THE INTERVIEW

RAYMOND: "I hear some good things about you from one of my partners. You come with excellent references. I remember when your dad, Carlos, may he rest in peace, used to come in and order only rice and chick-en, his favorite, every Tuesday like clockwork at 5:30 p.m."

JESSICA: "Thank you."

RAYMOND: "What made you pick Chorizo?"

JESSICA: "I heard this was the best restaurant to work for."

RAYMOND: "You heard right. Let me tell you what I'm looking for. I need someone who is going to be a team player. We work as a team in this restaurant. If one person slacks off or upsets one of our customers, we all suffer. My business suffers."

JESSICA: "I'm willing to do whatever it takes to be successful."

RAYMOND: "I've heard that before. There have been a lot of girls who have worked here and couldn't keep up. What makes you think you'll succeed where others have failed?"

Jessica uncrosses her leg briefly, revealing she has no panties on. Raymond's eyes are like the shutter of a camera. He never misses anything. He tries to maintain a businesslike manner. He quickly looks away and then responds to her.

RAYMOND: "Of course, there is a lot of room for growth here at Chorizo. It's entirely up to you. I take care of all my people. I promote all my people from within."

JESSICA: "Well, what do I need to do to move up rapidly in your organization?"

Raymond excuses himself and turns to the door, locking it from the inside. He comes back and returns to his seat.

RAYMOND: "I can offer you a position as hostess."

JESSICA: "Hostess or assistant manager?"

RAYMOND: "I have to ask you not to tell anyone about this rapid promotion. This is between you and me. I don't want any gossip among my crew. I'll bring you in with experience under your belt. I'm taking a big chance on you. Don't disappoint me."

JESSICA: "I promise you I won't."

RAYMOND: "It's your move, sweetie. What are you going to do for Raymond?"

Jessica uncrosses her legs, spreads both legs apart in a relaxed position. Raymond unbuttons the top button on his shirt and pulls his tie off. Jessica removes her blouse and drops it to the floor. She pulls her skirt up higher, closer to her crotch. Raymond at this point is breathing heavily with a noticeable bulge in his pants. Jessica removes her skirt and turns around in the seat, with her behind in Raymond's face. She removes her bra and tosses it behind her. It lands on Raymond's face.

Raymond has already removed his pants and dropped his underwear to the floor. He moves in behind Jessica and enters her. Raymond pushes in and out of Jessica with ferocity. She hangs onto the chair as it creeps close to the door. With each thrust that Raymond makes into her, she lets out a loud moan. Under one of her moans she manages to ask, "Does this mean I got the job?"

Two months into my Manhattan business, Frances pays me a surprise visit. She grew up in the same neighborhood, but became heavily involved in drugs. Frances went from being a burned-out crack addict to looking like a babe. She managed to clean up her act and went to school to become a counselor. Frances heard about my new restaurant and wanted to stop by on my birthday. I managed to convince her to ride home with me after work. I decided to stop for a drink at the local den.

I figure if we had enough drinks, I could convince Frances to come home with me. I thought I locked my front door when I got home, did not pay much attention to it. My mind was occupied with Frances. I had a room upstairs with a heart-shaped bed, Bose stereo system, a brick of coke, and a full bar. After five drinks, we both floated up the stairs to the fourth floor. When I opened the door, to my surprise Blanca was standing there buck naked on the bed. She yelled, "Surprise!" Blanca started to sing a happy birthday melody. That only lasted a few seconds before she realized what I had in mind. When she saw Frances, Blanca jumped off the bed like a wild beast before my eyes could blink and attacked Frances by pulling her hair and biting her face. I tried to separate them, but Blanca became more enraged. She smacked me, then reached over by the bed, got something sharp, and stabbed me on my side. The following day I called my therapist Psychic Cindy about giving me some kind of protection to keep this space cadet Blanca away from me and my business.

PSYCHIC CINDY: "Hello?"

RAYMOND: "Cindy, hi. This is Raymond."

PSYCHIC CINDY: "Hey, what's going on, love? How are you?"

RAYMOND: "Right now I'm hurting a little."

PSYCHIC CINDY: "Why? What happened?"

RAYMOND: "One of my ladies poked me in the side."

PSYCHIC CINDY: "You were stabbed on your side? Who did this?"

RAYMOND: "Blanca."

PSYCHIC CINDY: "Blanca stabbed you?"

RAYMOND: "Yeah, you can call it that. Caught me off guard."

PSYCHIC CINDY: "Are you all right?"

RAYMOND: "It's a little sore sometimes, but I'm fine."

PSYCHIC CINDY: "What did you do to this woman?"

RAYMOND: "You know me—I get along with everyone. This girl is a little mixed up in the head. She thinks that she owns Raymond."

PSYCHIC CINDY: "Now, Raymond, you know there's a lot of bad girls out there. There are a lot of good ones, too. You need to treat the ones that take care of you with respect and not treat them like the bad girls. The girl that stabbed you, you need to be very careful with her. Stay away from her. Looks like you're going to have to watch your back."

RAYMOND: "Yeah, that's what I wanted to ask you about. I'm calling you for some of your protection baths and candles."

PSYCHIC CINDY: "Okay, Raymond, I can do this for you. It will take me a while to prepare the bath and candle for you. Remember, Raymond, once you start these baths, do not stop until you are in a good place."

RAYMOND: "Good place?"

PSYCHIC CINDY: "Yes, Raymond, only you can tell. Use your senses. The same feelings that brought you to me. I'm preparing a special prayer that must be said while the candle is burning. Make sure you follow the instructions."

RAYMOND: "I don't know what I would do if not for you. I don't know why these things keep happening to me. I have nothing but love for my people. Why would anyone want to hurt Raymond? I treat everyone like they are family."

PSYCHIC CINDY: "Well, Raymond, you need to be nice to the ladies. Stay away from the wild ones."

RAYMOND: "They won't stay away from me."

PSYCHIC CINDY: "You must find some time to say a prayer, Raymond. Mother Mary will protect you. She can't protect you if she can't hear you. If you make time for her, she will help you."

RAYMOND: "I trust in Mother Mary, but I also trust a nine millimeter."

PSYCHIC CINDY: "Raymond, do you really think that weapons are the only way you can protect yourself?"

RAYMOND: "Not to put a fine a point on it, but yeah."

PSYCHIC CINDY: "Weapons only lead to more weapons. The best protection is the power of prayer. Of course, you need to watch your back as well. Stay away from Blanca. She's bad news, Raymond. She is not a nice woman. Don't forget to follow the instructions for the baths. I'm going to have it all typed out for you."

RAYMOND: "Thank you, Cindy. Raymond got your back."

PSYCHIC CINDY: "I got my own back, Raymond, but thanks, anyway."

RAYMOND DECIDES TO BACK OFF ON THE LADIES FOR A WHILE AND CONCENTRATES ON HIS BUSINESS

My two restaurants were so successful that I decided to open a third one in Maine. This would be a prime location for me. The focus with this restaurant would be in the area of entertainment. Every movie star and popular singer knew this location .They knew that Raymond threw the best of the best parties. I was becoming very well known among the elite crowd. I took care of them and they loved me for it.

I finally found a lady I absolutely adore. Margarita was my right-hand woman. She handles everything and lets me be my own man. Margarita understands me better than anyone and never gives me any pressure.

Song, "Black Magic Woman"

Raymond feels so confident with Margarita that he decides to stop the protection baths and candles. He calls Psychic Cindy to stop her from sending him more baths.

PSYCHIC CINDY: "Hello?"

RAYMOND: "Hi, Cindy, this is Raymond."

PSYCHIC CINDY: "Hi, Raymond, how are you?"

RAYMOND: "I'm doing good. I have finally found a good woman who loves and works with me."

PSYCHIC CINDY: "That's wonderful news, Raymond. Sounds very positive. Who is this woman?"

RAYMOND: "Her name is Margarita. I know you'll like her. I'm in a good place. You can stop sending me the baths. I don't need them anymore."

PSYCHIC CINDY: "Are you sure, Raymond? You should continue them to be sure. At least for a little while longer. What about the other woman named Blanca? Have you heard from her?"

RAYMOND: "I haven't heard anything from her. She's history."

PSYCHIC CINDY: "Okay, Raymond, but please watch your back. Don't let that guard down."

RAYMOND: "No, I'm fine. Thank you, Cindy. I'll be fine."

FROM THE MIND OF RAYMOND

It's been two years, and my business is going great at all my locations. I get a surprise visitor one night. While I'm counting out, my staff is changing their attire and picking up their tips. My head waiter, Marco, decides to play a song called "The Sea of Love." Our evening couldn't be mellower.

As I lose myself in the song, I hear someone say, "How you doing, baby?" Already in a good mood, I have this love smile on my face. When I turn to see who's talking, I realize its Blanca. My smile changes to a face of fear. I told her that I was getting ready to close and wanted to know what she wanted.

She motioned to me that her business there would not take much time. As Blanca walked close to me, I started to sweat from nervousness. I kept thinking in my mind of our ugly and brutal relationship.

Blanca leaned down at me and asked me to forgive her. She told me how sorry she was and that it was me she truly loves. As she approached me to give me a hug, my waiter Marco came over. Marco informed me at that moment that Margarita called and is waiting for me with a surprise.

40

Upon hearing this, Blanca pulls away from the hug. She gives me this surprise smile and says she is glad that I have found someone and wants to wish me good luck. I was hoping that Marco would pick up the look of panic that I had and get security. Blanca leans over and gives me a good luck kiss on the cheek. She motions to the door to exit and I follow her to lock the door behind her.

Halfway to the door, Blanca turns around with a knife in her hand. Before I have time to digest her intentions, I am stabbed at least nine times. Like a video movie in pause, my staff is in shock at what they see and are frozen in fear. With blood oozing out of my wounds, all I could think of was getting away from this lover-turned-assassin.

The funny thing about being mortally wounded is what people tend to think about at that moment. All I could think about was what was going to happen to my business. I had a lot of appointments that had to be met. Who was going to open up in the morning? What about the deliveries? There were a lot of other restaurants out there that would love to see me fail. This could not be happening. I just couldn't believe that I, Raymond, could be taken out by some crazed broad. Where did I go wrong? How could I have allowed anyone to sneak up on me this way?

I feel a sudden chill throughout my body. My legs start to give out from under me. The loss of blood saps my strength. I fall back from lack of strength to do anything .Blanca soaks the knife with the blood from my wounds and writes on my chest, "Raymond and Blanca forever." She forces a kiss to my lips and then slashes her own throat. Blanca wraps her arms around me and collapses on top of me. Unwilling to do anything herself, Blanca lays on top of me dying, while I am in despair, sucking in every breath to stay alive. My staff finally snaps out of their shock and calls 911. It seems like an eternity lying on the floor. At that moment my mind fades in and out to thoughts of my lady Margarita. As I lie there too weak to get up, I can hear the sirens of the ambulance getting louder and louder as they come closer to the restaurant. The lights begin to dim as the ambulance arrives at the scene.... ...

GIRLS WILL BE GIRLS

As we stand there staring into each other's eyes, our bodies draw closer together. I reach out and place my hand behind her neck and gently guide her face toward mine. I press my lips against hers. She returns the kiss gently at first, then reaches for a second, more aggressive kiss. I reach out to unbutton her blouse. She begins exploring my body up and down, then pulls at my panty and nervously guides it downward over my hips. Our clothes seem to drop to the floor as the air becomes filled with the aroma of sex. Our bodies mesh together with the rhythm of lesbian love.

FADE TO FULL STORY

My name is Donna. I am a retired police detective. I now work as a personal trainer. It allows me to pursue my favorite passion: women. I especially love young Latina women. I love the type that carries that Jiffy Pop butt. I can't help myself but spoil the women I date. I buy them anything they want. I am the man in the relationship, and I treat them as my bitch.

I met Maria, the love of my life, while on vacation in Los Angeles. Maria was so beautiful. I decided right there and then that I had to have her. Because she was straight, I didn't know what her reaction would be. That was one of the things that attracted me to her. The smile that she gave me the first time made me weak for her attention. I responded with typical dyke-bar rap and eventually got her name and number. I pursued her with white lilies and a rose, which I sent to her job. She worked as a customer service rep at the Ramada hotel. We dated for a while, and eventually she became comfortable enough with me to hold hands in public.

When we became intimate, she was very aggressive. She is more aggressive than I expected. She likes to bite my nipples and leave scratches on my buttocks when we have sex. I liked this response and it was a turn-on at first. Much more into the relationship, I decided to respond to this with some of my own rough sex. I began to fist her to see how she would respond. In the beginning I used three fingers and watched her reaction to it. She fought it at first, but started getting into the rhythm of it. Eventually after the third or fourth time, I began to work my whole fist into her vagina. She was

43

getting turned on to it and loved the aggression behind the act.

The look in her face was priceless. When I eventually worked my whole fist in her, she moaned and screamed to orgasmic climax. She began to expect this as part of our sexual time together. With twist and turns of my fist I was able to control the amount and type of orgasms she had.

This, however, produced an aspect of our relationship that brought out a violent streak. Her aggression started to escalate to violence. I was the man in the relationship, but I was also 110 pounds, five feet, four inches, and only had but so much strength. Her aggression, it was clear, went beyond a sexual one.

It was at this time through a close friend that I was able to seek the help of a talented psychic by the name of Cindy. With baths and special candles recommended by Psychic Cindy, I was able to bring some calm to Maria.

Things couldn't be any better for me. I was dating a woman I absolutely adored, and we were having great sex. About a year into our relationship, Maria decided to start dating a man name Derrick who worked with her at the hotel. She was still confused about her sexuality and was not 100 percent sure that she was gay.

DONNA SEEKS A COFFEE CUP READING FROM LONGTIME FRIEND PSYCHIC CINDY

PSYCHIC CINDY: "What's on your mind, Donna?"

DONNA: "Can you do a reading today for me?"

PSYCHIC CINDY: "What kind?"

DONNA: "Coffee reading."

PSYCHIC CINDY: "Okay. Decaf or regular?"

DONNA: "Uh…"

PSYCHIC CINDY: "Just teasing. Just take a minute."

Cindy passes a cup to Donna to sip a tablespoon of coffee. With a few minutes of various techniques, Cindy is examining the residue patterns that are left on the overturned cup. As she looks at the patterns, she speaks to Donna and reexamines the patterns.

PSYCHIC CINDY: "I see a man in your path."

DONNA: "You know me. A man?"

PSYCHIC CINDY: "Not a man for you. But there's definitely a man."

DONNA: "I'm careful about everything I do."

PSYCHIC CINDY: "Yes, but you're not here because of that. Someone's hurt you? Your heart is broken?"

DONNA: "I was so blind."

PSYCHIC CINDY: "What were you blind about? What caused this blindness?"

DONNA: "I don't know."

PSYCHIC CINDY: "You can't always see everything that's coming at you. You just can't."

DONNA: "It's not that."

PSYCHIC CINDY: "She has been unfaithful to you."

DONNA: "You might say that."

PSYCHIC CINDY: "I see a woman as well, and she is confused."

DONNA: "But what's happening to me is freaking bullshit."

PSYCHIC CINDY: "This woman destroyed you emotionally. I see she dumped you for another lady?"

Donna hesitates to answer .Cindy looks at Donna's eyes. Her years of experience in these matters have made her a keen detective of body language.

PSYCHIC CINDY: "It's a woman that separated you two. It's a man. She dumped you for a man."

DONNA: "Yep."

PSYCHIC CINDY: "I know this is going to sound kind of weird. It's not as bad as it looks."

DONNA: "How do you figure that?"

PSYCHIC CINDY: "That's what I'm reading now. She didn't leave you because of you. She left because she's confused about her identity."

DONNA: "Huh?"

PSYCHIC CINDY: "She needs time to figure out where she fits in. I don't want to give you false hope now. I'm not saying she's coming back.

45

Readings are never 100 percent. It could take a while. Or it may not happen."

Cindy looks at the patterns on the cup again. The patterns have taken on a different shape. She decides to hold off on this pattern message. The patterns show a woman behind a locked door. Cindy places the overturned cup upright on the table, signaling the end of the session.

DONNA: "It was a shock to me."

PSYCHIC CINDY: "Absolutely. It's always a shock. You love this woman a lot. I hope you're not planning on staying home and moping all day. Go out and try to have a good time. Believe it or not, you need a break, too."

DONNA: "I guess you may have a point."

PSYCHIC CINDY: "Yes, I do. I'm always looking out for you. Maria's friend pushed the man to her. Don't forget that. If you start feeling blue, call me. Anytime."

DONNA: "Okay."

Within the time that Maria was rediscovering herself, I started to date again and go back to the scene I knew best. My favorite dyke bar was a place called Uno's. There was no other place in the city that had this many gorgeous lesbians bumping and grinding to music.

I was in no hurry to replace Maria. I was still depressed from our abrupt breakup. Through many sleepless nights I went home with lots of women, removed lots of underwear, and nearly wore out my tongue licking vulva. I still had the bite marks on my breast from Maria. Maria had left many scars on my body. The scar that bothered me the most was the one on my heart. I had finally fallen in love and wasn't aware of it until now.

One day Maria decided to show up at my apartment. When I allowed her in, she became violent and started pounding at my face and chest. Maria was aware of my Uno's escapades and was not happy with me.

SCENE: DONNA'S APARTMENT.
DONNA AND MARIA ARE ARGUING ABOUT DONNA'S INDISCRETIONS.

MARIA: "What is this sh*t I heard about you and some bimbo at Uno's?"

DONNA: "What are you talking about?"

MARIA: "I'm talking about the bimbos you been bringing home from the club. You don't think I know? Everything that goes on at Uno's, everyone sees it."

DONNA: "I only went home with one girl."

MARIA: "Bullshit. That's not what I heard. Don't lie to me, Donna."

DONNA: "So, what's the big deal? You're running around with some dick. What do you expect me to do? Wait for you? I needed the company. I wasn't going to wait for you to decide what you wanted. You know I love you, baby. Come into my arms, baby. I need to hold you."

Everyone at Uno's knew each other's business. They knew Maria and me as a couple. At the same time Derrick, the man she was seeing, was getting suspicious. He was suspicious that Maria was involved in a relationship. He figures her for a straight woman. Derrick figured she was cheating with another guy. He decided to follow Maria on another one of her surprise visits to Donna's place.

Unknown to Maria, Derrick was also seeing someone else on the side. That person had followed Derrick to Donna's apartment to confront Derrick.

With his body pounding with adrenaline, Derrick kicks the door open to find Maria and Donna buck naked in each other's arms. Maria yells out, "Derrick! You followed me here? You bastard!"

While Derrick stands there in shock, Derrick's lover, who was following Derrick, walks in. Donna yells, "Who the hell are you?"

He says, "I'm Bobby, Derrick's boyfriend bitch! Who the f##k are you?"

"I'll show you who I am, asswipe!" Donna says. A melee ensues:

Derrick moves toward Maria. Donna moves to defend her and jumps in Derrick's face. Derrick swings wildly at Donna, Donna ducks and kicks Derrick in the groin, knocking him down to the ground. Meanwhile Derrick's boyfriend, Bobby, attacks Donna. Maria defends Donna and jumps on Bobby's back, scratching his face, blinding him, causing him to fall to the floor. There are so many bodies on the floor at this point; it's hard to tell who's hitting who.

The police arrive at the scene, and everyone is arrested and taken in. The group spends the night in jail, the men separated from the women.

47

The group is charged with disturbing the peace. They are given a slap on the wrist, and twenty-four hours later everybody is released from jail.

EPILOGUE:

Because of the showdown at my apartment, Maria has a rude awakening. While we were locked up at the jail, Maria reminded me that she belongs to me and only me.

MARIA: "You took a big chance getting in Derrick's face. What made you think you could take him?"

DONNA: "What was I supposed to do? Don't you know by now how I feel about you? I would never let anyone hurt you. Not anyone. No man could ever come between us. Only a woman knows how another woman feels. From the very first day I saw you, I knew."

MARIA: "You knew what?"

DONNA: "I knew that we were meant for each other."

It's been ten years, and Maria and I are happily married.

Song: "Be My Baby."

MY ALIBI

In a backroom of a storefront lit by a flickering light bulb, a thirty-five-year-old man with dark shades and body piercing is slamming a young, scantily clad girl against the wall and slaps her when she speaks back to him.

HUGO: "What the f@%k is wrong with you? I told you before, when you blow a Jon make sure he pays you first. Don't let me remind you again, you stupid bitch! Now get the f*^#k out of my face and go make me some money."

FADE TO FULL STORY

Rachel was the sweetest girl in the world. She had such a hot body. I always got a hard-on when she was near me. I never mess with the girls after they start working for me. Rachel had the potential to make me a lot of money. She was young, and could be with me for many years. The problem with Rachel is she is as smart as a pet rock. The slaps I gave her should keep her awake for now. I didn't want to do too much damage to her, otherwise I will lose money. I let her go with a warning.

HUGO: "Next time I'll cut your f*#king face!"

My name is Hugo; I live in the Red Hook section of Brooklyn, where I own a string of businesses that hide my crack cocaine business. I own a barber shop, as well as a strip club I call *My Alibi.*

Today was like every other day. After picking up supplies for my barber business, I found out one of the girls who works for me at my bar was sick. I needed to replace her fast. Time was money, and I love money more than time.

When I arrived at the bus station, I found a schedule for all out-of-state trips and pretended I was waiting for an arrival, to blend in to the crowd. I could always spot a runaway and had become good at it. Most of these girls were tired, hungry, and confused. A good meal and a place to lay your head down weren't easy to turn down.

This is how I met Elyse. She was from Chickasaw, Alabama. Elyse arrived looking thin and hungry. She was young and attractive, big hips, and nice-looking breasts. I convinced Elyse to have lunch with me. After gaining her trust, I told her I could provide her a job with good money. She was interested. Afterwards I brought her to a private room at my lounge, *My Alibi.*

I gave Elyse everything she was missing from home and more. I made her one of my bitches, and now she was going to do anything for me. This girl was going to make me a lot of money.

Everything was going smooth for me. The barber shop was bringing in steady money. My crack business was increasing, and I had plenty of women. But something was missing in my life.

Denise moved into my neighborhood from the Forest Hills section of Queens. I always made it a point to know anyone who moved on to the block. This girl drew my interest, so I finally introduced myself.

She had a big butt, and her hair was long and smacked her butt as she walked. Nothing turned me on more than a girl with long hair and a nice butt. I invited her out to eat and tried to be as cool as possible. I just couldn't take my eyes off her butt. Every opportunity I got, I looked. To be cool, I wore shades to hide my eyes.

After two weeks of dating, I get a call from Denise. She invites me over her apartment for dinner. I never waited two weeks for sex. Whenever I wanted sex from a woman, I took it! Why was I allowing this woman to control me like this?

When I arrive, Denise opens the door in a micro denim skirt and a T shirt with no bra. She doesn't need a bra. Her breasts are so erect, I almost salute them. She plants a kiss on my lips and tongues me briefly. My rod goes from limp to erection in record time. My coolness is gone; I now have a telling bulge in my pants

DENISE: "I'm so glad you're here, Hugo. Do you want to eat first? Or f**k first, then eat later? After we have some rough sex, we can eat."

FROM THE MIND OF HUGO

This surprises me, so I stand there speechless. Denise makes the decision for me and reaches down, looking for my penis. She smiles and unbuttons my fly, pulls down my zipper. My penis pushes its way out to freedom. Denise drops her skirt and panties to the floor. She grabs my penis and guides it to her crotch. She rubs the tip of my penis against her orifice. By now I'm leaking sperm all over her leg, and about to burst.

Denise has me locked in with a firm grip on my erection. She finally wakes up from her trance and we make our way to her bedroom. She lies down on her stomach with her butt up in the air. I enter her behind and start pumping myself to an eventual orgasm. The harder I pump, the louder she screams.

I slip a few times and come out by mistake.

DENISE: "Don't you dare come out, Motherf*^Ker! Put it back, put that f**king c**k back in!"

While I'm still inside her, I turn her over on her side and slide my hand under her crotch and begin to rub her vulva. By now I can sense by my throbbing erection that she's having multiple orgasms. As I continue to rub, her moaning is getting louder. I react to her movement and synchronize my rubbing with her movements. When Denise finally reaches her peak, her body gives off one big body shake. We reach orgasm together and collapse from exhaustion.

SEVERAL YEARS LATER:

I was bringing in three grand a week with my crack business alone. Between my lounge and barber shop, I was able to clear about five grand. The barber shop and lounge were my legitimate businesses. As the businesses grew, I needed to think about having a partner I could trust. I started by asking Denise to watch the girls when I was out moving dope. She was good with the girls and had a big appetite for money. My money was now her money, so I knew she would take care of business.

HUGO: "Denise, what's the total on Rachel for the night?"

DENISE: "Rachel brought in about eight hundred last night."

HUGO: "Not bad. Looks like the slaps in the face turned her around. Have to hit her harder next time. Keep an eye on her."

DENISE: "Why? What happened?"

HUGO: "Bitch tends to forget to collect her money first. She been blowing Jons for free. Just keep your eye on her. Have Elyse work the overnight tonight. She's real good with the Jons all day. Let's see how she does with the overnight crowd. Get CeCe to cover her day shift."

DENISE: "Little CeCe."

HUGO: "Yes, that's right, little CeCe. I also want China Doll working with CeCe: I need to bring the lounge up to six or seven grand. I may need more bitches. Denise, remind me to call my mother tonight."

DENISE: "Okay, baby."

HUGO: "Don't forget to pick up my Devil Dogs when you go to the supermarket. Bring me back five boxes of Devil Dogs. Did you hear from Lollipop yet?"

DENISE: "Not yet."

HUGO: "You have her number?"

DENISE: "Yeah, one sec."

HUGO: "Call her. She should be here already. Gonna have a talk with her. Tell her to see me as soon as she comes in."

FADE TO OFFICE OF PSYCHIC CINDY

Cindy's assistant, Bebe, is whispering to Cindy over the telephone.

ASSISTANT BEBE: "Cindy, I have a scary-looking guy out here. Says he has no appointment with you. But he still wants to see you."

PSYCHIC CINDY: "Scary-looking?"

ASSISTANT BEBE: "Kind of gangster-looking. Says his name is Hugo."

PSYCHIC CINDY: "Hugo, yes, tell him to come in."

Hugo is reading a handyman magazine, but behind his shades his eyes are all over Bebe's body.

ASSISTANT BEBE: "Mr. Hugo, Cindy will see you now."

Hugo walks in and takes his shades off.

PSYCHIC CINDY: "Well, Hugo, this is a surprise! What brings you all the way here?"

HUGO: "Hi, Cindy, it's been a long time. Nice place you have here. This is a lot bigger than the other place you had. Not to mention that nice honey you have working for you outside."

PSYCHIC CINDY: "You mean Bebe?"

HUGO: "Yes, she looks delicious."

PSYCHIC CINDY: "Bebe is a good kid."

HUGO: "Life is good."

PSYCHIC CINDY: "Yes, it is. I know you didn't come all the way here to admire my office, but thanks."

HUGO: "No, I came here to get a reading. The kind of reading that only you can give. I have a lady now."

PSYCHIC CINDY: "Oh?"

HUGO: "I've been with her for a while now. Business is good now, more than good. I need to know if she's trustworthy."

PSYCHIC CINDY: "You want to know if you can trust her after, what, three years? Let me get this straight: you want me to tell you its okay to trust her? You know I won't do that. You know her better than me. It's never a sure thing."

HUGO: "What do you mean by that?"

PSYCHIC CINDY: "She may be trustworthy today. Tomorrow brings no guarantee. Can I see your palm?"

HUGO: "What took you so long?"

PSYCHIC CINDY: "How long has she been with you?"

HUGO: "'bout three years."

PSYCHIC CINDY: "But three years ago she wasn't involved in your business as she is now."

HUGO: "That's right."

PSYCHIC CINDY: "Well, sounds like you trust her enough to keep her."

HUGO: "She handles my girls when I'm not around. Knows the flow of the house."

PSYCHIC CINDY: "If you have a good woman, take care of her. She'll take care of you. I can't tell you how anyone is going to behave as your business grows. Big money sometimes brings out an element of greed inside a person. Sometimes there's no effect at all. Everyone reacts different. Keep your eyes open and your ears sharp."

HUGO: "Should I keep Denise involved with my business?"

Cindy examines Hugo's palm.

PSYCHIC CINDY: "Again, that's your decision. You've been with her for three years and your business has grown. I'd say that says a lot right there. It's been three years and nothing bad has happened? This is one of those moments where you have to trust your heart. I don't think it's her you need to worry about. I see there will be a lot of confusion and danger coming around you! Don't let money dull your street sense."

HUGO: "Can I bring her with me next time so you can read her?"

PSYCHIC CINDY: "Absolutely. I welcome the both of you here anytime. I'd like to meet her. See my assistant Bebe on your way out. She'll ink in the appointment. Don't be a stranger now."

Being around Denise, I thought a lot about expanding my operation outside of Brooklyn. She had a lot of friends and family in Queens and, as I got to know them, I began to expand my business to the streets of Queens. I hired two runners who have been with me for some time and promoted them to security positions.

Fat Boy Al was a kid from Flatbush Avenue. He loved to eat, but was very fast on his feet for his size. We called him El Gordo. Al was a brilliant kid whose parents wanted him to stay away from us. He loved the action of the street and had a keen sense of organization. The other soldier I use is Mike the Cut Man. Mike and I went to the same school. We grew up in the same neighborhood. He dropped out of school and started using dope. Mike's favorite hobby was knives, and he quickly gained a reputation for being the most dangerous white boy in our neighborhood. He lost his parents in a car accident. I took him in when he was only fifteen and he's been with me since. Mike was more dangerous cutting someone then using a piece. He always carried both.

Saturday night was pickup night. My dope was running low, so I made arrangements to pick up new dope at our buy place, the handball courts off Lincoln Terrace, Crown Heights, in Brooklyn. I was carrying $150 grand, so my soldiers went along to cover my back. I left Denise back at the lounge in charge of the girls.

We walk in through the gates and up the stairs leading to the upper handball courts off Lincoln Terrace. With my eyes scanning, I notice two soldiers standing on either side of the bag man. Fat Al is on my left and Louie on my right. I always pack my iron when picking up dope. This was pretty much routine for us, except this time something's different. I could not place it, but my instincts are giving me signals.

As we move closer, it seems like time slows down. Then it hits me! The gates to the courts are locked. These gates are never locked. It's a setup! I motion to my soldiers to abort, but it's too late.

Al and Louie instantly draw their weapons and aim in the direction of the bag man.

Out of nowhere a dude pops up with an AK-47 weapon about to open up on us. I reach to my belt for my nine and point straight at him, firing into his chest. I let off seven rounds. He's stunned but not going down.

What the?

I look at my gun and then realize, *Blanks!* I have nothing but *blanks* in my gun!

THE POTION

Things seem to be going well for me and Eric. He was into bondage and loves to tie me up with heavy ropes during sex. He positions me on the bed, face down, and spreads my legs apart. He ties my hands and feet to the bedposts. Eric would then pull out a whip and smack me on my butt with it. While doing this he would repeat the words "Who's your daddy? Who's your daddy?"

FADE TO FULL STORY

My name is Melissa. I am a twenty-four-year-old event planner living and working in Manhattan. I've been going out with Louie for over two years now. Several months ago I found out that he was cheating on me. At first, I began to be in denial about Louie's carnal appetite. He left so many clues around that I couldn't take it anymore. The pressure was too much for me. One night I flipped out on him.

The next thing I knew I was in the hospital with both wrists severely cut. My arms were bandaged, and I had an intravenous bottle attached to my left arm. My advisor Psychic Cindy, who is a therapist to me, came to visit me at the hospital.

FROM MELISSA'S BED AT ST. LUKES'S HOSPITAL

While Cindy holds Melissa's hand, Melissa is just opening her eyes from a nap.

MELISSA: "Cindy. How did you find out about me?"

PSYCHIC CINDY: "Louie called me and told me what happened."

MELISSA: "I'm just so ashamed of myself. Everything just happened so fast. I mean, next thing I know I'm here."

PSYCHIC CINDY: "The important thing now is that you heal."

MELISSA: "I don't want to go through this again. I can't do this, Cindy! What's wrong with me?"

PSYCHIC CINDY: "Absolutely nothing that can't be fixed. This will pass. It's going to make you stronger."

Melissa: "Do you think I'm a loser, Cindy?"

Psychic Cindy: "Of course not. You are one of the warmest people I know. You're only a loser when you quit! Right now I see a survivor."

Cindy relaxes her grip on Melissa's hand and pauses before she continues. She sees another man in Melissa's life, but also knows that her life with Louie is not over.

Psychic Cindy: "You're a strong woman, Melissa."

Melissa: "Not when it comes to Louie, though. I'm afraid. You see, Louie has a way of getting to me."

Psychic Cindy: "Ya think?"

Melissa: "He isn't the best-looking man. He doesn't even take care of himself. He's overweight and sloppy. This really drives me nuts sometimes. But he does have gentleness about him. That makes up for everything else. That is something that I've never had with any other man."

Psychic Cindy: "That's not why you're here, Melissa."

Melissa: "Well, it's not his fault. I know that now. He comes in sometimes with this perfume smell on him. Not my perfume— somebody else, some other woman."

Psychic Cindy: "I don't want you stressing over this right now.

Melissa: "It's okay, I need to talk about this. Louie came in from work and we had a big fight."

Melissa recalls in her mind the night of the fight with Louie.

FADE TO FIGHT SCENE BETWEEN LOUIE AND MELISSA

Melissa is doing the laundry for Louie and about to throw one of his pants in the washer. She feels a bulge in the pockets and sticks her hand in to clear the pockets. She pulls out a pack of Trojan condoms. She starts to throw them out in the garbage, and then she changes her mind and puts them in her own pocket.

That evening when Louie comes home from work, she meets him as he comes in the door. Melissa throws the pack of condoms and hits Louie in the face with them.

Melissa: "What the f*ck is this shit?"

LOUIE: "F#ck, what the hell is wrong with you, woman?"

MELISSA: "You lied to me. You told me that you changed. You told me that you weren't going to play me anymore. Why did you lie to me, Lou?"

LOUIE: "I don't know what you're talking about. Those condoms are old. I had them there for months."

MELISSA: "I don't believe you. I washed those pants last week, and that pocket was empty."

LOUIE: "Maybe you didn't see them."

MELISSA: "That's bullshit."

LOUIE: "You know what? Now I remember. Those condoms are not mine. I'm holding on to them for a guy that works with me."

MELISSA: "Which guy?"

LOUIE: "I can't tell you that."

MELISSA: "You can't tell me because you made it up. I suppose you think I'm imagining that perfume smell you have on, too."

LOUIE: "That's my aftershave, woman."

MELISSA: "That isn't aftershave, asswipe. I know the difference between aftershave and perfume. That's f#cking perfume!"

Lou's eyes bulge out and his eyebrows rise up. With a sudden rage he grabs Melissa by the throat and presses her against the wall.

LOUIE: "Listen, bitch. I told you they're not my condoms. Why do you have to continue with this shit?"

Louie is such a big man that Melissa is overcome by his strength. She manages, however, to kick him in the groin.

Louie releases his grip as he collapses in pain to the floor. Melissa runs to the bathroom and locks herself in. Still in pain from the kick, Louie decides to leave the apartment to cool off and comes back an hour later. When he comes in, he realizes that Melissa is still in the bathroom.

LOUIE: "Honey, I'm sorry about what happened before. I promise I'll make it up to you. Honey, can you hear me? Are you all right, honey? Lissie, open the door."

A panic look takes over Lou's face as he begins to replay the fight scene and wonders if his attack did more damage than he imagined. With no response from Melissa, Louie pushes the door open to find Melissa collapsed, blood oozing out of both her wrists.

BACK TO SCENE AT ST. LUKE'S HOSPITAL WITH PSYCHIC CINDY

MELISSA: "I don't remember what happened after Louie left. All I know is when I opened my eyes, I was here. They told me I tried to hurt myself. I don't remember that."

PSYCHIC CINDY: "You need to get plenty of rest. When you get well, come and see me. I have some special baths just for you."

SEVERAL MONTHS LATER, after recovering from her ordeal

FROM MELISSA'S MIND

When I recovered from my wounds, I decided to try to forget about Louie and met Eric. Eric was in the military, twenty-seven years old, and very nice-looking.

We have been dating for a while. Everything seems to be going great. We always look forward to being in each other's company. One day, however, I make an important discovery. Eric has been taking strong bipolar medication. I decided to confront him about this. Eric is very upset over my discovery and boldness. He becomes very abusive, both verbally and physically.

MELISSA: "Eric, I need to talk to you about something."

ERIC: "Okay. What's up?"

MELISSA: "These pills—I found them in your closet."

ERIC: "What pills?"

Melissa pulls out a jar of pills from her purse.

MELISSA: "These."

ERIC: "Why are you going through my stuff?"

MELISSA: "You didn't tell me you were taking meds."

ERIC: "You stupid-looking bitch! Since when do I have to tell you my business?"

MELISSA: "Are you serious?"

ERIC: "Yeah, I'm serious. Does the look on my face look like I'm not? Stay the fu* k away from my stuff!"

Eric moves over toward Melissa and snatches the bottle of pills out of her hand. He shoves her away from him. She falls back and lands on her butt. He kicks her all over her legs and pulls her hair.

ERIC: "Get up, bitch! Get the f*ck up now!"

MELISSA: "Stop it, Eric, stop kicking me! You're hurting me!"

ERIC: "Don't look at me like that, asshole."

He hits me so often I have welts all over my body. It seems we couldn't have a discussion without him becoming physical. I have had enough.

I'm nobody's punching bag. Eric and I eventually broke up our relationship. The last time I was going to see him, he left me waiting for him at a park bench.

One thing led to another, and somehow I was back with Louie. How could I be sure that Louie would stay with me? And not hit me? More than anything else, I needed the security of having a man around. I decided to seek the help of a Gypsy Woman. This lady assured me that what she had in mind would guarantee to keep my man passive and in love with me. That was what I wanted. If a man was in love with me, I figure he'd stay with me. How could I turn this down?

Gypsy Molina wanted me to bring her a cup of my urine the next time I had my period. I thought it rather strange, but I was desperate and complied. Later on, I found out this was known as "Italian Sauce."

Three weeks later I delivered my cup of urine blood to Gypsy Molina. She advised me that the potion would be ready that night about 7 p.m. I picked up the potion with instructions to mix this with any sauce into Louie's dinner. Gypsy Molina said it would take a few hours for it to start working.

The next night I slipped the potion into spaghetti sauce that I made and put it aside, making sure that Louie got a healthy portion. I nervously waited for about two hours. Louie had fallen asleep in his recliner, thank God, when he suddenly got up.

Without saying a word, Louie headed out the door. I wonder if this was part of it. Maybe Louie needed some air. I was so nervous that I was shaking.

About fifteen minutes later, I got a knock on the door. I figured it was Louie, so I opened the door. To my surprise a tall, dark-haired, handsome man was standing there with a strange look on his face.

MELISSA: "Who are you?"

DAVID: "Don't you know me? I'm the love of your life, David!"

David even knew my name, which really took me for a spin. He placed me in his arms and told me that he couldn't live a day without me. This was either a dream or someone was playing a joke on me. My phone was ringing. When I answered it, it was Gypsy Molina. She said that she accidentally mixed my potion with someone else's and that she was hoping to get me in time.

MELISSA: "This can't be happening!" You crazy f*$#king b@#ch! What am I supposed to do now?"

Gypsy Molina explained that it would be about four days before the potion wore off. Louie had ingested a potion from another woman, One Eye Sara, and was now madly in love with her. The spell filled with her scent of urine would drive him to her. I had no other choice but to now entertain a man name David who was convinced that I was the woman of his life. His lust for me was maddening and unconditional.

MEANWHILE *LOUIE* ARRIVES AT ONE EYE SARA'S APARTMENT

Louie nervously rings the doorbell. One Eye Sara, thinking its David, opens the door without looking through the peephole.

LOUIE: "Hi, baby, did you miss me?"

ONE EYE SARA: "Who the hell are you?"

LOUIE: "Don't you recognize me? It's Louie, your sweetheart."

Sara's cell phone begins to ring;

ONE EYE SARA: "Could you hold on a second while I see who this is?"

GYPSY MOLINA: "Sara, there's been a mistake with the potions."

ONE EYE SARA: "What mistake?"

GYPSY MOLINA: "The potions were mixed up by accident, I'm afraid."

ONE EYE SARA: "It can't be! What about David?"

Sara realizes why Louie is at her apartment. She is livid at this point and strains to remain calm in the midst of her newfound admirer.

One Eye Sara: "Lou, baby, I'll be with you in a sec. Can't you do something, Molina?"

Gypsy Molina: "It will only last for about four days; then things will return to normal."

One Eye Sara: "Four fu*king days? You must be kidding! I have to entertain this fat bastard for four days?"

MEANWHILE BACK AT MELISSA'S APARTMENT

We floated around naked in my apartment and had mad sex .What was I supposed to do? Here was a guy who was gorgeous and crazy about me no matter what, so I went with the moment! On top of that, he was hung like a thoroughbred racehorse.

Molina was right! About four days later, David woke up and was confused about where he was. I thought it best not even to try to explain anything to him. I led him to believe that he picked me up and we had a one-night stand. I explained to him that I had a boyfriend who lived with me and he left quietly. I can't deny that we had a great time together. And I was beginning to think that maybe this happened for a reason.

Louie returned about two hours later and told me that One Eye Sara had explained to him about the spell. Like a tornado Louie started tossing things around and cussing under his breath about crazy fu#king women. Eventually he calmed down but somehow the potion took a toll on him. He was never wrapped too tight to begin with, and now he was worse than before.

That night when Louie and I made love, all his hatred came out. I tried to fight him off but he somehow managed to snap a bone in my neck. I was put on life support, with a machine to help me breathe. I could hear my therapist, Psychic Cindy, saying a prayer for me as she held my hand.

EPILOGUE

Louie is on the run from the police for domestic violence. He winds up back at One Eye Sara's place. She is shocked but somehow allows him to stay with her. One Eye Sara has a soft side for Louie because of her own personal experiences. She harbors him from the police until Louie can figure out his next move. David finds out about Melissa and rushes to the hospital to find Psychic Cindy by her side.

MY TUTOR

OPENING SCENE

Avery sexy girl wearing only a fireman's hat with her back to the pole moves her hips back and forward from side to side and around in a circular motion. With the fireman's pole behind her, she then does a full slide to the floor and teases the firemen by bringing her knees up and down. She then does a full split. The firefighters are ecstatic that Paulie has chosen to entertain them, giving them this Christmas/New Year's gift.

FIREFIGHTER VASQUEZ: "Yo, Paulie, where did you find this honey? Can I take her home after this?"

PAULIE: "Only if you can afford her. She's not cheap."

FADE TO OPENING SCENE

My name is Paul and I'm a volunteer fireman for Ocean County. I've been a fireman for five years. I'm married and I have a seven-year-old boy. Up to five years now, my life had become routine. One day all this changed when I became involved with the daughter of one of the men I work for.

My attraction for Claire Sawyers began when she was seventeen-years-old. When she turned eighteen, my attraction for her was brought to a whole new level. It started one day when I was helping her with her homework at the firehouse.

CLAIRE: "I swear, I just hate school!"

PAUL: "What's the matter, sweetie?"

CLAIRE: "I hate school. I can't seem to understand this work."

PAUL: "Can't you get your old man to help you?"

CLAIRE: "He said ask your mom, and she said ask dad."

PAUL: "Let me take a look at it."

CLAIRE: "Would you really?"

PAUL: "Sure, let me see what I can do for you."

CLAIRE: "That's so sweet of you, Paulie."

For Claire it was a big thing that Paul would go out of his way to help with her homework when no one else would. Paul didn't know it, but it made Claire look at him in a whole different way. She thought of Paul as a hero because no one else would help her. Her infatuation with Paul began to build. Of course, when Paul realized how she began to think, he was unsure how to handle this eighteen-year-old.

The firefighters lived in a two-story building, and the upper level was where they stayed when it was time to relax. On one occasion Claire's father, Brian, comes upstairs and walks in as Paul is helping Claire.

BRIAN: "Hey, Paul, what's up?"

PAUL: "I'm helping Claire with her homework. Do you mind, Brian?"

BRIAN: "No, not at all. Thanks, Paul, I appreciate that. When it comes to math and stuff like that, I got to tell you—I was really bad with that when I was in school. My wife, she don't have the patience you need for it. She don't read too well, anyway. That's so nice of you."

PAUL: "Hey, man, anything for a fellow firefighter. After all, we are one big family. We take care of our own."

FADE TO PAUL AT THE FIREHOUSE CLEANING EQUIPMENT AFTER DUTY

At first Paul thinks he is imagining things. Every so often he would catch a glimpse of a man several feet away from him. As Paul turned his head to look, the figure would vanish. Paul figured he was tired and his mind was playing tricks. Then the sights became more vivid and longer before disappearing. Finally one day Paul turns his head and gets a full glimpse of his sighting. His heart starts to race as he realizes that it's himself he is looking at.

The man he sees looks exactly like him. This twin of Paul is staring at him with a smile. Paul starts to perspire, as he is frightened and can't tell if he's awake or it's a bad dream.

PAUL'S ALTER EGO: "Well, what are you looking at?"

Paul's eyes open wide, as he can't believe what he sees. He turns around to see if anyone is behind him.

PAUL'S ALTER EGO: "Yes, you. I'm talking to you, Paul."

PAUL: "How can this be?"

PAUL'S ALTER EGO: "How can what be?"

PAUL: "You can't be real."

PAUL'S ALTER EGO: "Oh, I can assure you, I am very real."

PAUL: "Why are you here now? I've never seen you before."

PAUL'S ALTER EGO: "I'm here because of you, fool. I'm here because of the opportunity that is coming your way."

PAUL: "What are you talking about?"

There was no answer and the entity that look exactly like Paul vanished as quickly as it appeared. Paul figures he must be having some kind of aftereffect from all the smoke that he inhales on the job. He makes it a point to get out and get as much fresh air as possible. Paul avoids talking about this to anyone. This could lead to a disability leave of absence if it gets out.

If anyone even saw Paul talking to himself, he would have to see the company shrink. Paul thinks he just had a moment of madness and forgets about the whole incident.

FADE TO SCENE WITH PAUL AND CLAIRE DISCUSSING HOMEWORK

CLAIRE: "Paulie, can you please help me with my bio homework?"

PAUL: "What kind of questions you have for me?"

CLAIRE: "My teacher says she wants us to write about pheromones. Do you know anything about pheromones?"

PAUL: "Well, yes. Pheromones is chemicals that animals and humans give off when there is attraction."

CLAIRE: "How do you know what it smells like?"

PAUL: "It's not something that you can smell like a regular smell. It usually comes on by contact or some other kind of stimulus."

CLAIRE: "You find me attractive, Paulie?"

PAUL: "You're very attractive."

CLAIRE: "Do you think I give off pheromones?"

PAUL: "I'm sure that you do, Claire."

CLAIRE: "My dad always says that I'm fat."

Claire places her hand over Paul's hand and gives him a look of infatuation. Paul's alter ego suddenly appears out of nowhere. Paul is shocked beyond belief. He thought he had seen the last of this double.

PAUL'S ALTER EGO: "She's kind of cute, huh, Paulie?"

PAUL: "Oh, no, it's you again! Do you know she's only eighteen?"

PAUL'S ALTER EGO: "She's barely legal. Go get her, boy!"

CLAIRE: "Paul, who are you talking to?"

PAUL: "Nobody. Just thinking out loud."

Paul feels torn about leading young Claire on with her infatuation. Their homework sessions continue, and Paul finds himself for the first time looking forward to them. His ego twin encourages him to see Claire as much as possible. It now has changed from a tutor session to a young girl teasing an older man. Paul's alter ego always seems to appear whenever Paul is with Claire.

Claire has decided she wants to be with Paul outside of homework. She decides that the next time they meet she will invite him to the movies. Paul is on level two of the firehouse. He decides to take a nap.

A couple of hours later, he feels a hand running through his hair. He opens his eyes to see Claire staring down into his eyes.

CLAIRE: "You have such nice hair."

PAUL: "Claire, you scared the bejesus out of me!"

CLAIRE: "I'm sorry. You look so peaceful. I just couldn't help myself."

PAUL'S ALTER EGO: "Did you hear what she said, Paulie? I think you have a shot at this ass."

Paul, not wanting to blow his cover, keeps quiet. He hears his alter ego but won't answer.

PAUL'S ALTER EGO: "I guess you're not going to answer me."

CLAIRE: "Paul, do you want to go to the movies with me?"

PAUL'S ALTER EGO: "This is your chance, Paulie boy. Don't blow it. You do, I'll never go away."

PAUL: "Sure."

PAUL'S ALTER EGO: "'Atta boy, Paul, looks like you're finally going to get some tail."

SCENE WITH PAUL IN THE CAR WITH CLAIRE AFTER THE MOVIE

CLAIRE: "Thanks, Paul. I had a good time."

PAUL: "It's late. I should get you back home."

CLAIRE: "It's okay. I told my dad I went out with some friends. Could we sit here for a while? I don't want to go home just yet."

PAUL'S ALTER EGO: "This is your chance, Paul. Don't screw this up. I thought it was kind of sneaky of you to park on the roof level."

CLAIRE: "Are you okay, Paul? Why are you looking at me like that? Do you like me, Paul?"

PAUL: "Of course I do."

CLAIRE: "I want to be close to you. I'm still a virgin."

PAUL'S ALTER EGO: "You hear that, Paul?"

CLAIRE: "I'm waiting for someone special."

Paul leans over to Claire and meets her lips with his. She is surprised at first, but responds by wrapping her arms around him. They share saliva as their bodies take over the moment. Paul is startled as he hears his alter ego.

PAUL'S ALTER EGO: "Now that's what I'm talking about! I have hope for you yet. This is your moment, Paulie. Don't screw this up now. Its booty call time, brother Paulie babes."

As things heat up, Claire reaches down and grabs Paul's crotch. She begins to rub and squeeze him. The more she rubs, the harder he gets. Paul responds by unbuckling the button on her pants. He slides his hand down between her legs and works his finger along her private.

Within minutes their clothes are off, and he turns her around and enters her with great force from behind. She lets out a scream of pain and then moans of pleasure. Paul hears his alter ego chanting for him.

PAUL'S ALTER EGO: "Pump that booty! Pump that booty! Pump that booty!"

The windows of the car are now fogged up as Paul explores every orifice of Claire's body. They stay there for over two hours sharing their body fluids. This rooftop love nest becomes routine and convenient for them. They meet and have sex in the car several times a week.

PAULIE AND THE OTHER FIREFIGHTERS GO OUT AND MEET AT THE BAR FOR A DRINK. CLAIRE's FATHER, BRIAN, AND PAUL ARE IN A CORNER TALKING ABOUT THE UPCOMING COMPANY HOLIDAY PARTY.

BRIAN: "What should we do this year?"

PAUL: "I got a few ideas."

BRIAN: "I bet you do. Maybe something the boys haven't seen. Something different."

PAUL: "I promise it will be good."

BRIAN: "By the way, Paul, Claire's grades have improved. Great job! Take as much time as you need with her. I can't thank you enough."

PAUL: "It's my pleasure, Brian. Claire is such a sweet girl."

Paul's wife, Amanda, suspects that her husband is having an affair. She hears from her older friends that the woman Paul is seeing is a young girl. Out of embarrassment, she breaks her ties with most of her older friends. She doesn't know who to trust. But she knows firefighters are a tight group of families. Her need to know who this young woman is is overwhelming. She decides she needs a spy. Behind her friends' back, Amanda asks Eileen Sawyer's daughter to spy for her. She meets with her at a local diner.

AMANDA: "Thanks for taking the time to meet with me. I really need your help."

CLAIRE: "Sure. I'm happy to help you."

AMANDA: "This is going to sound hard. I need you to spy on my husband."

CLAIRE: "You mean, Paul? Spy on Paul? Why?"

Claire catches herself and then realizes that she needs to sound less surprised about Paul.

AMANDA: "I think he's seeing another woman. A young girl."

CLAIRE: "What makes you say that?"

AMANDA: "It's going around town. Look, I'll pay you for it."

CLAIRE: "I don't know about this."

AMANDA: "I'll pay you double."

Claire figures she better take the offer, otherwise Amanda might get suspicious.

CLAIRE: "Okay, okay, I'll do it."

AMANDA: "One more thing."

CLAIRE: "What's that?"

AMANDA: "Don't mention anything to your mom."

FADE TO THE OFFICE OF PSYCHIC CINDY, SATURDAY 3 P.M.

AMANDA: "Cindy, I'm so glad that you could see me. Paul is just so out of control. I feel like I don't even know him anymore."

PSYCHIC CINDY: "Okay, let me see what's going on. Get all the energy out and into the cards."

AMANDA: "Cindy, he don't even come home sometime. When he does, we just end up fighting."

PSYCHIC CINDY: "Okay. What can I do for you today?"

AMANDA: "Can you give me a reading with tea leaves instead of the cards?"

PSYCHIC CINDY: "I can do that. You sure you're okay with it?"

AMANDA: "Why?"

PSYCHIC CINDY: "You may not like the results."

AMANDA: "Don't care. Do it."

PSYCHIC CINDY: "Okay. I see a child in the future. A little girl."

AMANDA: "A little girl?"

PSYCHIC CINDY: "I didn't say yours. It is in your path."

Amanda forms a routine of seeing Psychic Cindy every Saturday. Most of her sessions are a way for her to vent her frustrations.

ONE OF MANY MEETINGS AT AMANDA's HOUSE WITH CLAIRE

AMANDA: "Have you got anything on Paul's girlfriend?"

CLAIRE: "All I know is she's from outside the neighborhood. Someone he met at a strip bar. Some erotic dancer."

AMANDA: "Did you get a name?"

CLAIRE: "Not yet, but I'm working on it."

AMANDA: "What's that? You brought something?"

CLAIRE: "Just something I picked up on my way over here. You really want to know?"

AMANDA: "Yeah, I do."

Claire opens her package to reveal a box containing a double dong.

AMANDA: "What the hell is that?"

CLAIRE: "It's something for pleasuring yourself."

AMANDA: "But it has two sides."

CLAIRE: "You wanna try it?"

Amanda is surprised but also has suddenly become aroused at the sight of this huge double dong lesbian erotic device. Amanda is surprised at her actions as her hormones seem to take over. She finds herself removing her clothes. As Claire massages her with the dong, Amanda becomes more aroused and excited at the idea of having sex with a woman.

Claire is taken to the bedroom by Amanda. Claire inserts the bigger end of the dong into Amanda and the other end into her. Amanda moans as Claire rocks forward and back giving pleasure to her and herself.

The two women rock their pelvis' back and forth .As they come simultaneously, they hold on to each other, locking their lips together. As they suck each other's saliva, the bed begins to reek of sex. The air is filled with orgasmic moans and screams. There is no end to their ongoing orgasms.

What was supposed to be an hour-long meeting has now turned into a pleasure fest without regard to time. They are so engrossed in their pleasure that they don't hear the jiggling of keys at the door. Paul opens the door and hears the sounds of moans coming from the bedroom.

With a look of "now I got her," Paul quietly moves toward the door expecting to catch his wife in bed with another man. He opens the door quickly. With a look of shock, he drops his keys.

CHAPTER THREE
GUYS AND DOLLS

I like to parade around in my iron panties and dance for Charlie. It excites him to see me in this way. My panties have a keyhole where the crotch is. Charlie had this made especially for me. He dug this contraption up from some obscure sex shop downtown. It makes him feel that he is in control, and that my vagina belongs to him alone. Charlie, my correction officer boyfriend, has a fetish about locking things up. Before I allow him the key to my panties, he must make love to Mary. Mary is a full-size functional doll with all the parts of a woman. Watching him having sex with this doll stimulates me so much I can feel myself getting wetter and wetter. "Make love to her Charlie, like you would make love to me," Chrissy tells him.

Charlie takes Mary and positions her on the bed and spreads her legs apart. He positions his penis into her. At the same time he begins kissing her, Chrissy lies alongside him and Mary and begins stimulating herself. Chrissy's face goes from pink to red as she begins to lose herself to climax.

FADE TO FULL STORY

My name is Christine and I like to play with toys during my sex. I'm forty-eight years old and work at the Comfort Inn Hotel. I met Charlie at the motel one day and we've been together for over two years. I see a lot of men at the hotel, but the only one who caught my eye was Charlie. He is the first man to keep me involved in his life. Charlie, like me, is married. Charlie has five children and a wife he's been with for ten years. Charlie makes it no secret how much his wife hates him. His wife hates him so much; she curses the ground that he walks on.

On Fridays from 2 a.m. to 7 a.m. Charlie and I always have breakfast together and then great sex. Until Charlie met me, he forgot what great sex was all about. He shows his gratitude by showering me with love and attention.

Charlie likes to play the role of the dominant one in our relationship. He sat up one night and created what he called Christine's Bill of Sexual Rights. At first I thought he was just kidding and I took it as a sick joke. Charlie printed it up and hung it over our bed.

When I make love to Charlie, he always starts off by reading me my rights. He wraps my hands behind my back and puts the cuffs on. He grabs me and throws me on the bed and enters me from behind. While he's humping he recites the words:

"You have the right not to have an orgasm until I tell you.

"You have the right to my sexual desire, or fantasy.

"You have the right to entertain me sexually.

"You have a right to engage in sexual acts of my kind.

"You have a right to be in my private sexual fantasy."

While Charlie is giving me my rights, my sexual sweat is pouring down my legs. By the time he's finished, I've had multiple orgasms and I'm ready to continue playing. Once my hands are free, I bring out my own bag of toys to share in our sexual fantasy play. We now enter our private world of fantasy.

Charlie's favorite toy is penis candy. I use the cherry flavor one and lay it on the tip of Charlie's penis. It drives him absolutely wild while I enjoy the cherry taste. My favorite flavor is Piña Colada. I usually bring along prolong spray but after using the head candy, Charlie doesn't seem to need it.

The sex is good, but it isn't just the sex that keeps us going. Sometimes we meet for brunch or just to hang out and catch a good movie. It is always an adventure for us. If there isn't anything to do, we find something to do. One time we rode the subway down to Coney Island and hung out there for the entire day.

As we go through our routine secret encounter, we're reminded that we do have a married life that we must go back to. Charlie's wife drains him financially every moment she can .She is only with him because of his kids. Charlie has the added pressure of supporting his family, while also having a girlfriend.

I needed to be sure that Charlie and I were meant to be together. There was also a part of me that wanted Charlie no matter what. Was Charlie my soul mate? I never pay too much attention to that word, but now it was important to me. I needed a reading to confirm any doubts that I had about Charlie. I was referred to a psychic by the name of Cindy.

CHRISTINE is on the phone with PSYCHIC CINDY's ASSISTANT

CHRISTINE: "Hello, my name is Christine Silica. I would like to know if Psychic Cindy is available for one of her special readings."

ASSISTANT BEBE: "Special reading?"

CHRISTINE: "The one they call the twin."

ASSISTANT BEBE: "Twin flame. One minute, let me see if Cindy is available to talk to you."

Bebe has been instructed to forward all special reading inquiries directly to Cindy.

PSYCHIC CINDY: "Hello, this is Cindy. Can I help you?"

CHRISTINE: "Hello, Cindy. I understand that you do twin readings?"

PSYCHIC CINDY: "Yes, I do. Why does it have to be a twin reading?"

CHRISTINE: "Don't know. I heard it is one of the best around. A close friend of mine recommended you."

PSYCHIC CINDY: "Do you know what a twin reading is? Or why it's called a twin? I ask you this because I want you to know what a reading like this involves."

CHRISTINE: "It has to do with my soul mate."

PSYCHIC CINDY: "Not exactly the same. There is a difference between a soul mate and a twin flame."

CHRISTINE: "Really? I imagine them both being the same."

PSYCHIC CINDY: "Soul mates are very familiar and comfortable lovers you had in previous lifetimes. A soul mate can even be the same sex. A twin flame is never the same sex. Twin flame is your other half."

CHRISTINE: "My other half."

PSYCHIC CINDY: "You only have one twin flame and soul mate. That twin is perfect in every way. Your souls are connected through a silver cord."

CHRISTINE: "Connected for life?"

PSYCHIC CINDY: "Yes, for life. That cord is severed at birth. Torn in half to occupy two separate bodies. This one person is perfect for you because you shared the same soul at birth. People spend an entire lifetime trying to reconnect with this twin. It even shares the same breath and heartbeat as you."

CHRISTINE: "I feel a presence sometimes in my dreams."

PSYCHIC CINDY: "That is the person who is perfect for you in all ways. You would have the perfect relationship. That person feels the same way about you. When I read you, it will give you accurate insight into who this twin is."

Christine is all ears and likes what she hears about the reading. In her mind she begins to fantasize about what it must be like to have the perfect relationship. She is counting on her twin being Charlie.

Deep down inside she doesn't have the heart to ask, but Cindy is way ahead of her. The twin flame reading doesn't quite work that way.

Cindy understands that clients sometimes try to fit their lovers into the mold of the twin flame. Psychic Cindy stays on the line and continues to answer questions about the twin flame reading process.

CHRISTINE: "What are the chances that my twin flame is someone that I'm already involved with?"

PSYCHIC CINDY: "There's always an exception to every relationship, no matter how in love you are. A twin flame is not abusive or selfish. They are not drawn together based on ego or lust or intense physical attraction."

CHRISTINE: "What draws them together, then?"

PSYCHIC CINDY: "They are drawn together for the common good. They don't engage in any behavior that is of a destructive nature. To answer your question, they are drawn together by true love and respect. A person who truly respects you will never lie to you."

CHRISTINE: "Is that why I hear the word *soul mate* so often?"

PSYCHIC CINDY: "The term *soul mate* is used carelessly without its true spiritual meaning. More often than not, it is used to disguise an artificial relationship."

CHRISTINE: "When can I have this reading?"

PSYCHIC CINDY: "Anytime you're ready to start. It takes about three days to complete."

Unsure that the reading will point somewhere else other than Charlie, she puts the twin flame reading on hold until she can gain enough courage to stare at the truth. The one thing she is sure of is that she wants Charlie closer to her.

Christine decides to rent an apartment only two blocks away from where she lives with her husband. If you avoid the devil, you will always run into the devil.

Unknown to Charlie, Christine also has a dark side to her. She loves Charlie and there isn't anything she wouldn't do for the man she loves. With Charlie, she believes that one day she will settle down. She will let nothing get in her way of that goal. There is only one thing stopping her, Charlie's wife, Lisa.

Christine is tired of hiding and decides that she will confront Charlie's wife about their relationship. To avoid getting Charlie upset with her, she decides not to tell him of her plans to meet Lisa. Christine meets Lisa at her home while her kids are away at school. Lisa thinks she is meeting with Charlie's private insurance carrier. She has no idea who Christine is.

CHRISTINE: "I'm not who you think I am. I had to tell you that to make sure you would see me."

LISA: "Well, who the hell are you?"

CHRISTINE: "I am Christine. I've been seeing Charlie for some time now!"

LISA: "So you're the bitch that my husband's been f*@king! You must be insane! You got a lot of f**king nerve, bitch!"

CHRISTINE: "Hold on, I didn't come here to fight. I'm just tired of the masquerade! I just want to make him happy! Can't we be adults about this?"

LISA: "I'll tell you what I can be. I'm going to court Monday and file charges for infidelity. I'm also going to file charges against the f**ker for child abandonment. He'll be lucky if he's allowed to see *photos* of his kids! Is that adult enough for you?"

CHRISTINE: "You can't be serious?"

LISA: "If that's not enough, I'm going to up his support money to the max. Are you aware that he has five kids to support? Maybe you're the sixth kid! Honey, you don't know who you're f##king with!"

CHRISTINE: "Okay, you know what? It doesn't matter what you do. Charlie and I are going to be together no matter what! There is nothing you can do about that—nothing!"

LISA: "Get the f%$k out of my house, bitch!"

Lisa throws a table lamp at Christine, barely missing her head. Christine, startled, jumps away and continues out the door. As she is heading out she can hear Lisa kicking the furniture and trashing the house in anger.

Christine's emotions are all over the place. At the same time she feels a sense of relief that everything is out in the open. The following day she meets up with Charlie at her apartment.

Charlie comes in and has a look of tension on his face.

CHRISTINE: "What's wrong?"

CHARLIE: "It's Lisa! She was found late last night in her car shot to death! I was on my overnight shift at the jail—"

Charlie is distraught and can barely continue.

CHRISTINE: "Who did this?"

CHARLIE: "I don't know, haven't told my kids yet. I don't know what to do."

Christine holds Charlie in her arms, and they fall asleep. Several hours later, there's a knock on the door. She awakes.

Christine looks through the peephole and sees two police officers.

POLICE: "Mrs. Christine Silica? This is the police! Open the door."

CHRISTINE: "Charlie, get up! There's two cops outside my door."

CHARLIE: "Well, let them in."

The officers come in and ask:

POLICE: "Are you Mrs. Christine Silica?"

CHRISTINE: "Yes. "

POLICE: "You're under arrest for the murder of Lisa Bengetti."

The police read her her rights and, while Charlie looks on in shock, she is handcuffed and led away.

CHARLIE: "Don't worry, honey, we'll fight this! I'll get my lawyer and have you out soon."

With no effort to fight the arrest, Christine is led away and placed in the back of the police car. Charlie is still shocked by the events that have unfolded and stands there in disbelief. Before the car pulls away, Christine tells the officers, "You think you could make these handcuffs tighter? They feel better when they're tighter."

Chili pepper

I started working at *Club Excuses* to supplement my income. It soon became a lot more than a part-time job. Pole dancing isn't easy. You have to be in top shape to even stay on the pole for a few minutes. They call me the Chili Pepper because of my explosive sexual nature.

At first I didn't recognize him. I see a lot of men all night and I never expect or think that I'll run into someone from my other job. This time I did. Max worked in the produce department at Wholesale World. Trying to appear unnoticed, he crept up close to the stage. I decided that I was going to give him a view of me that he only dreamed about at Wholesale World.

With my back to Max, I bend over with my head down to the floor and wiggle my butt close to his face. He is so close to the stage, I could feel his breath hitting the back of my thigh. I grab the pole and swing around while holding my legs spread apart as I rotate around the pole. I am giving him a private show but he's either too dumb or too cheap to acknowledge it. I decide to crawl up near him and spread my legs wide in his face. He pulls out a five spot and nervously positions it under my thong. I turn around on my knees, hands to the floor, and push my butt within inches of his face. I want him to smell the sweat from my crotch. I push what I'm allowed to do to the limit. While the music is playing, I'm moving to it back and forth in Max's face. He is frozen in excitement and within seconds of bursting at the seams. This is the kind of sexual power that I crave, giving me my mini orgasms as well.

FADE TO FULL STORY

My name is Chili. I'm forty-nine years old, soon to be fifty. I work at Wholesale World and have been there for five years now. I also work part-time at a strip joint in Manhattan called *Excuses*.

The first man I met at Wholesales was Steve. Steve is tall, dark, and extremely handsome. I loved having Steve's black skin up against my white skin. It turned me on fiercely. My favorite place for sex was at work in the meat cooler.

OFFICE OF PSYCHIC CINDY, 2 P.M. WEDNESDAY

PSYCHIC CINDY ON THE PHONE WITH HER ASSISTANT

PSYCHIC CINDY: "Who is next on the list, Bee?"

ASSISTANT BEBE: "It's your favorite person."

PSYCHIC CINDY: "Chili is here?"

ASSISTANT BEBE: "With her dogs. One of them already peed on the carpet."

PSYCHIC CINDY: "Oh, no!"

ASSISTANT BEBE: "I told her we don't allow dogs in the waiting area. She insisted that you are okay with it."

PSYCHIC CINDY: "Bee, tell her to put the dogs in the back room before she comes in to see me. You know, the supply room. And call Carlos— tell him I need a spill cleaned up. Thanks, Bee. Send her in as soon as that's done."

Wearing black patent leather boots and skin-tight pants, innocent-looking but never naïve, Chili walks in a half hour later with a beaming smile.

CHILI: "Hello, Cindy."

PSYCHIC CINDY: "Well, hello, Chili. You look very happy today."

CHILI: "I'm always happy."

PSYCHIC CINDY: "Not like today. And I see you got your hunting boots on."

CHILI: "You never know who you might run into."

PSYCHIC CINDY: "This is true. What brings you to me this afternoon?"

CHILI: "Cindy, I need a controlling bath."

PSYCHIC CINDY: "Controlling bath plain or with honey? The boots are not working? Just teasing you! Before I forget, Chili: you need to leave your dogs home. I can't have them ruining my carpet. I have other clients coming in as well."

CHILI: "But they don't like to stay home alone."

PSYCHIC CINDY: "You're always welcome, but the dogs can't be here. Now, as far as your bath...I can get a bath ready for you in four hours."

CHILI: "I've been going back and forth with Steve. But now he's just getting on my last nerve. Sometimes I want him in the worst way. He just isn't there for me."

PSYCHIC CINDY: "Careful, Chili, you're steaming up this room! What brought all this about?"

CHILI: "You know how I like my dark Mandingo warrior?"

PSYCHIC CINDY: "Yeah."

CHILI: "The other day I was in the cooler."

PSYCHIC CINDY: "The meat cooler? You were in the meat cooler with Steve?"

CHILI: "All 175 pounds of him! We worked up enough heat to warm up the entire store. I just couldn't get enough of him. I was wondering what it would be like to have him all the time. We have sex at least three times a week! Then I thought about your controlling baths. What I wouldn't give to have him all the time!"

PSYCHIC CINDY: "I can prepare this kind of bath for you. That's not a problem. But it comes with a warning label: Be absolutely sure you want this man unconditionally."

CHILI: "You know I like my meat dark!"

PSYCHIC CINDY: "Yes, I do. I'll have that ready for you by Friday."

CHILI: "I knew I could count on you. You're the best. By the way, there was this guy out there in the waiting room staring at me."

PSYCHIC CINDY: "I wonder why. You're not exactly dressed like you're going to church."

CHILI: "He is kind of cute."

PSYCHIC CINDY: "There you go again! Don't forget I'll have that by Friday."

I made sure there was plenty of light on in the cooler. I wanted to see Steve's black circumcised penis. The greatest feeling for me was to have hot sweaty black and white sex in a cool environment. Because of this cooler sex, I developed a reputation I didn't ask for. I changed my name from Chili to Chili Pepper. Steve would piss me off by reminding me that he was all about sex. I didn't mind having sex with him, but I didn't like it being thrown in my face that it was all about sex with him.

I grabbed fruits and started to pound him with it, and the tall bastard started getting off on it. I decided to tease him by coming in one day wearing thigh-high patent leather boots with my hot red miniskirt. I hadn't spoken to him for two days, and I could see his excitement through his pants. Part of his excitement was that he knew that I dress this way for him. I purposely walked by him and pretended to lose my footing and let my butt hit his erect penis. I then walked away from him. I could see the sweat coming out on his forehead.

During my small time away from men, I would visit my therapist Psychic Cindy every three weeks. She would prepare and customize one of her famous love and honey baths. This would make me like honey to bees. The men being the bees, of course! Every man who came in contact with me wanted me. What more could I want?

I made a lot of trips to the cooler with many different men. The man I like the most was Dave. Dave was Puerto Rican, dark-skinned, married but separated from his wife. What Dave lacked in size he made up for in technique. These Spanish men were like Viking warriors. When they had sex with you, they turned you over for hours and hours. Having sex with Dave made me so hot I couldn't think of anything but feeling his meat inside me. Dave loves to enter me and then pick me up and walk around the room with him inside me. Sex was not just an adventure for him. He made me feel like whatever he was doing, he was doing it just for me. I told Dave I prefer a man with a smaller organ. It made him feel so comfortable, he pushed me to the floor, spread my legs. He ate me till my orgasmic fluid shot out and squirted him in the face.

On one occasion, while having crazy anal sex with Dave in the produce room, we accidentally knocked over a damaged box of cucumbers. As I approached to pick up the box, I noticed its spilled contents. Underneath the cucumbers were bags of white powder. Dave helped me put the boxes back in order and advised me not to mention it to anyone. Dave said he knew what was going on but wasn't involved in it.

I discovered the operation and didn't know who to trust and who not to trust. The operation was in the product returns. The drugs were brought in through a regular delivery. The cocaine was stuffed in plastic bags and return bags placed on top of them. The buyer would then make arrangements to pay for the drugs. The money was placed in the security room and held there until goods were verified by the buyer. The money was always kept in a backpack. Steve and Kenny, the security guards, were in charge of this and held the money in a locked cage.

Once the buyers arrived, they were taken to a back room to examine the cocaine. This took about fifteen minutes and was the only time Steve and Kenny left their post.

Once the payment was made, the pickup of the drugs was made as a regular pickup of return goods. This would make the transaction seem to be a normal part of wholesale activity. Money from drugs stashed into produce amounts to four to eight million dollars in transactions.

Manger and other personnel were involved in this cocaine business. One big weakness in this drug operation was no video cameras were scanning the security area where the money was kept. This was purposely done to avoid any recorded activity in the event they were busted. That was smart, but also dumb. It was only a matter of time before someone took advantage of the lack of video.

Oops, but I'm getting ahead of myself. After all, how could a dumb blonde like me figure out any kind of scheme like this one?

There were two other weak links in this operation, Steve and Eddie. I know Steve and I knew that I could distract him enough to leave his post long enough for that money to disappear. The only time both men left together were when the buyers were there to examine the goods. Eddie was our garbage guy, and he was pretty much on time. If he was late with the garbage pickup, the plan would fail. At any given time there was at least six million dollars there. The code word that was used over the PA for the delivery was "customer special order." Steve always disappeared to the back when this announcement was made. This announcement was always made on Tuesday at 6 p.m.

One recurring thought occupied my mind. There was enough money in one of the money bags to be set up for life. I would never have to work at the strip joint or work at Wholesale again. This Chili Pepper was going to be set up for life. I would be celebrating my fiftieth birthday in Spain.

Many thoughts occupied my mind. How could I get at the money? Where would I stash the money? Could I avoid exposing myself? I knew I had to get into that room.

It was Monday and I wore a low-cut blouse, no bra, and low rider jeans. It was easy to get Steve hard up and ready for some cooler sex. I grabbed at his crotch and told him that I wanted him bad. I pulled off his pants and without him noticing, slipped his keys off the key clip and tucked them under my clothes. I gave him oral like it was my last day on earth, and afterward rode on top of him like a cowboy gone mad. I gave him my "Chili Pepper Special": around the world. I sat on top of him with him inside me and spun around 360 degrees, rotating and squeezing and holding his penis with my insides. Steve held out to the very end and knew when I was close to orgasm. The sexual sweat and odor from this movement was enough to make us both come. I wanted him to go into a deep sleep after sex. I held him close to me and waited till he fell asleep.

I had ten minutes to get dressed and run across the street, make a copy of the key, and get back to Steve before he woke up. On my way out I ran into Alfred, my department manager, and told him that I was on my ten-minute break. He looked at me strange and nodded okay. With only two minutes left, I returned to the cooler, placed the key back on Steve's key clip, and quickly undressed and returned to Steve's arms. The Chocolate lover was still asleep. Steve opened his eyes.

STEVE: "Spin me some more, baby. Spin me again."

CHILI: "Time to get back to work, baby. Maybe later?"

It was Tuesday and the only thing left was to make sure that the garbage be picked up on time. This would be crucial as to getting the money out of the building. Eddie would pick up the garbage from the cooler at 6:32 p.m. These were large 70-pound bags. The final bags were placed in the Dumpster by 6:40 p.m. From 6:15 to 6:30 was the grab time. There was no other time this could be done.

At 5:45 p.m., my supervisor decides to pick this time to pay me a visit. He tells me that he needs to talk to me about work in his office. My manager, Alfred, was always making passes at me whenever we were alone. Once we get to his office, he closes the door. Alfred tells me that if I wanted any kind of future here, I need to be open-minded. What he really meant was for me to take my clothes off. With my mind racing against time, I had no time to fight with him. I remove my clothes and decide to give him what he wants. With his legs spread out over boxes, I give him a slow and forceful oral pleasure. He was so huge I thought my mouth was going to rip apart at the ends. I could feel his penis pulsating in my mouth. His orgasm was imminent. He wanted to delay climax. I wanted him to come to climax so I could leave. While my mouth was busy, my eyes were on the clock on the wall. I grabbed his cheeks and squeezed them, sinking my nails into them. This was more than too much for him. I pulled my mouth off and he shot cum two feet past my head, landing on the floor. His reaction was to say, "F@%king bitch!"

With Alfred asleep in his office, it's now 6 p.m. Customer special order announcement is made over the intercom. The money has just arrived. Steve and Kenny are on their way to secure it. I pick up 20 pounds of mangoes and work my way back to receiving for a box. Moving a box of produce around a market was my regular routine. It would not draw any suspicion.

I scan around the facility and see Eddie making the rounds with the garbage. He should be in the cooler room on time.

6:14. I head toward the security cage with a box of mangoes and a large garbage bag inside. Steve and Kenny are with the buyers looking over their merchandise. The key is a perfect fit. I bag the money and dump it in the box, replacing it with mangoes. After locking the door, I head toward the cooler to fill the garbage bin with the money. I stuff the top of the bag with bad meat.

6:32 Eddie picks up the garbage from the cooler and heads toward the Dumpster.

EPILOGUE

Spanish maracas playing in background.

It's been one hour and I'm starting to fall asleep. Who would have believed that there was eight million dollars in that backpack!! I just couldn't leave it back there. I left Eddie a stuffed envelope in his locker. He should have gotten it by now.

The plane is riding so smooth you could barely tell you're in the air. I should be in Madrid in another three hours. The stewardess says that dinner in Madrid is usually served at midnight. I mailed my therapist Psychic Cindy a bonus check and sent it via Fed Ex before I left. I will be sending her a postcard from Madrid.

As the flight starts to make me sleepy, I enter a dream state and fantasize about my favorite hobby. One thought keeps going through my mind: "Spanish men! Oh, my God, I wonder what they're like in Madrid?!"

Chili is dreaming.

BUON APPETITO

C oats and empty hangers are falling down around us as we struggle to remove our clothes. I grab her around her hips, she spreads her legs apart, and I lift her up and move her pelvic against mine. As I enter her, she reaches out to keep from falling back and grabs a coat that slips off the hanger and crashes to the floor. We finally wind up against the closet door, where I start humping her against the door, trying to go deeper inside her. With each forward thrust I make, Lena's back crashes against the door, and my legs struggle to support both our weights.

FADE TO FULL STORY

My name is Manny. The ending of my twenty-year marriage with Carmen was also the beginning of my new life. This new life also was the beginning of Latin cuisine dynasty in New York. My new life started when I enlisted the help of a top advisor by the name of Psychic Cindy. We eventually became the best of friends.

My twenty-year marriage was at rock bottom. I began seeing a woman I met while interviewing applicants for a position at my social club, ACES. The craziest thing happened to me when it was time to interview Lena. Like a possessed soul, I was fixed into a trance. I had to have this woman. Lena would later tell me that she wanted me just as bad. Thus followed a long romantic relationship.

I could not believe what was happening. At the same time I felt rather guilty about the whole thing. I was not in the habit of seeing other women while married to Carmen. That is, until I met Lena. I decided to seek the help and advice of my longtime friend Psychic Cindy. I told Cindy that I had fallen for a woman called Lena. It was a love like I've never experienced before. I just can't seem to get enough of her. I need to know if this is the woman to enter my life and turn my life around.

Cindy advises me of the following. She tells me that tomorrow would be Yemya's birthday. She is goddess of the sea. This goddess opens and clears paths that are blocked. I was told to go to the ocean before sunrise and pray to her. Give her all my energy. I am a spiritual person as well, but not as strong as Cindy. By saying these prayers I could ask her for anything.

Cindy is on her way to the beach with her crew as well, but to a different location. I called Cindy and told her I was at Brighton Beach, Brooklyn.

Somehow I must have taken a wrong turn afterward and wound up in Coney Island. I walked around, then called Cindy. She advised me to go to the sand, sit, and pray.

It's 4:00 in the morning and I'm sitting in the sand waiting for the sun to come up. At this point I am so desperate for answers. I do nothing but think and breathe Lena. Please give me a sign. I need to know if she is the right one for me. I get up and walk to the water, where I wet my feet with the incoming waves. I ask for God to please show me a sign. As the sky lights up, I get up and start to walk toward the boardwalk. I look at my phone. It has one bar left—I forgot to charge it. As I am walking closer I see this sign on a restaurant. As I get closer it reads LENA'S! LENA'S, LENA'S, LENA'S.

It's been two years. The road that led to Lena my love also led me to begin a new business as well. I decided to close down the social clubs and partner with two other retirees from the police force. We decided to open the restaurant of all restaurants. This restaurant would feature Italian cuisine like no other. Entertainment would complement the aura of the restaurant. When it came to entertainment we would spare no expense.

MANNY SEEKS A DRAWING BATH
FROM HIS FRIEND PSYCHIC CINDY

Like a cat that's just eaten a mouse, Manny sits in the office of Psychic Cindy with a larger-than-life smile.

PSYCHIC CINDY: "Well, Manny, I have to say, you surprise me today!"

MANNY: "So do you. You have an assistant now? Piped-in music in your lounge. The soft life. Life's been good to you."

PSYCHIC CINDY: "Tell me how many cups of coffee you had today, Manny."

MANNY: "Maybe five, but that's not why I'm wired! Thanks for taking me without an appointment."

PSYCHIC CINDY: "To what do I owe this visit?"

MANNY: "Cindy, I'm so glad to see you. Besides your usual charms, I need your special skills. Cindy, can you make me one of your drawing baths? I need as much luck as I can get."

PSYCHIC CINDY: "Sure can. You seem very excited about something."

MANNY: "Well, yes, Cindy, I am. I'm in the process of starting a new business. I need all the luck that's available."

PSYCHIC CINDY: "I can feel the positive energy you're giving. As long as you maintain that, you'll attract positive things."

Unable to hold back his excitement, Manny reveals his plans.

MANNY: "I and a couple of the boys, retirees from the force, are opening up a restaurant. It is going to feature fine Italian cuisine."

PSYCHIC CINDY: "That sounds fabulous!"

MANNY: "As a matter of fact, I want you to be there at the opening."

PSYCHIC CINDY: "Well, Manny, I'm very happy for you. It looks like you're on your way to a good place. You definitely need a special bath that is going to not only bring you luck but cleanse the old away. You know, you have to follow these directions to the letter, otherwise it will spoil the bath."

MANNY: "Well, here we go again. You know I'm no good with stuff like that."

PSYCHIC CINDY: "It really isn't that hard. Come on, now, you done this before."

MANNY: "I know, I know. You know me—I want everything fast. You're right; I'll keep track of the steps."

PSYCHIC CINDY: "Yes, don't forget now…Each day a prayer must be said with the bath. I'm going to print that out for you. Seven-day bath, each day save a portion of the bath water in a jar. On the seventh day, you dispose of the bath in front of your house. I'll have the bath ready by the end of today."

MANNY: "You're going to be at the opening?"

PSYCHIC CINDY: "Of course, Manny. I wouldn't miss it for anything in the world. I enjoy seeing you happy and successful. By the way, Manny, I'm also including candles with the bath."

MANNY: "Cindy, my restaurant is going to make history. Italian cuisine will never be the same in New York. It will give Italian food a new level of acceptance and respect in the restaurant business."

As Cindy listens to Manny, she gets a feeling that grabs her attention. In her mind's eye she sees flashes of a war. In Cindy's vision she sees a war among Italian restaurants competing with each other. This cuisine war is competition for the taste of millions of New York customers. The profit potential is staggering. There are some casualties of this war as well.

She knows that in every business venture, there are always issues. It would serve no one for her to mention this at this time to Manny. Cindy knows that because of his Italian/Spanish heritage, Manny is well aware of how far the competition will go to stay on top.

Manny walks out of Cindy's office with an extra beat to his step as his ego is hyped with optimism. He now has the blessing of his psychic, and he feels good about the direction he is going.

Before we open our business, we sat down with an attorney. We agree to remain partners to the business, and all three of us would own the rights to the business if the business were to expand.

Its opening night at "La Famiglia" and everyone is there to celebrate and wish us good luck. My partner Vinnie the mouth and "JD" Joe Demetrio all added our special talents to the business.

Our business drew the best Italian crowd from all over the city. Celebrities were always at the restaurant. This gave the restaurant clout. It also drew some of the best-looking women around. One of them was JD's cousin Felicia.

Music Playing, Crowd Dancing

JD's cousin Felicia was always at La Famiglia. This thirty-two-year-old bubble-butt lady lived for the moment. She also had a hidden agenda as well. Felicia worked as a manager at a midtown bank. She was always hungry for the limelight and had a thing for Manny. Anytime Manny was there, she would show up. Manny was attached and had his own lady. If you knew Manny, you knew that women always flocked to his side. He had that kind of aura. JD was unaware of Felicia's attraction to Manny. He was too busy running the business to notice. The three partners had an unwritten rule. No one would mess with each other's family. It was all about family respect.

On his way to work, Manny finds a black rose with a note attached to his car. When Manny opens the note, it says,

To: Manny with all my love
Your secret admirer

Manny is hoping that Lena didn't see the note. He crumples up the note, and throws the black rose to the street. This is the first of many roses that are left on his car and doorstep.

One of the roses is found by Carmen's mother, Dominica. She suspects that Manny is already seeing another woman who is much younger. Dominica sees her daughter crying every day. She sees her daughter is always waiting for her ex-husband to return. She decides to take matters into her own hands.

Dominica attempts to keep Felicia away from Manny. She uses the same rose she found to conjure up her type of voodoo spells. The spell is an evil one against Felicia. Manny is unaware of the other forces that shape and control his future.

Felicia's best friend was a girl named Maria. Maria was all right as long as she wasn't drinking. Once she started drinking, her nymphomaniac side came out. Whenever Maria came to the restaurant, you knew there was going to be trouble. Felicia used Maria to avoid implicating herself directly in any evil doings. She saw Manny as an easy target. Felicia wanted Lena out of the way of her plans. The fact that she was also younger infuriated Felicia even more.

Friday night the business is doing a photo shoot and all the owners have to be around to promote the restaurant. Felicia shows up wearing the slinkiest, revealing, look-at-me dress. She takes a photo with all three owners and then has one taken with just Manny. Manny is with Lena, his woman. They mingle with the crowd. Felicia has been drinking heavily and she is starting to loosen up. After the photographers finish, they are invited to stay and enjoy the night. Felicia asks Eddie the photographer if he could shoot her alone in a private area .Felicia asks that her photos be taken in the nude. She strips down to her panties.

FELICIA: "Do you want to play a game?"

EDDIE: "What kind of game?"

FELICIA: "Take a photo of me like I am and make sure that it gets mailed to Manny's girlfriend, Lena. On the photo write: *"To Manny, now you can keep me forever."*

EDDIE: "I can't do that."

MANNY: "Oh, yes, you can. Come on, Eddie!"

Felicia reaches over and grabs Eddie's crotch.

FELICIA: "It's just a joke. No one else has to know."

Felicia pulls out a roll of money and places it in Eddie's hand.

EDDIE: "I'll see that it's taken care of."

FELICIA: "I have a little something extra for my Eddie."

She pulls his zipper down and encourages his already erect penis out of his pants. Felicia gets down on her knees and takes his penis in her mouth until she can feel it reach the back of her throat. She grabs both his cheeks and squeezes his butt. She licks his tip as he struggles to avoid going to orgasm too soon. The sensation of Felicia's aggressive hold is too much for Eddie and he finally lets go. Eddie opens his eyes and sees Felicia licking and swallowing cum off his tip clean.

Manny is alone at the restaurant one night going over the bills and drinking a bottle of scotch. He hears a tap on the glass. He opens the door and Felicia is standing there looking hot as ever.

FELICIA: "Well, aren't you going to invite me in?"

MANNY: "Felicia! What are you doing here? We're closed, you know!"

FELICIA: "It's okay. I came to see you anyway."

MANNY: "Well, I guess it's okay come in."

FELICIA: "What does a lady have to do to get a drink? Did you get my roses?"

MANNY: "Felicia, you know that you and I can never—"

Felicia stops Manny from saying anything further by placing her three fingers across his lips. She removes her hand and replaces it with her lips. Manny hesitates at first, but the alcohol he's consumed gets the better of him. With his inhibitions loosened, he answers her kiss with his own and his tensions are now gone.

As they peel off each other's clothes, they work their way to a back room. Manny grabs her, and ties her hands to the doorknob. He then spreads her legs.

Manny tells Felicia, "I'm going to teach you the alphabet game."

"The alphabet? I know my alphabet," says Felicia.

"I bet you can't recite to Z."

Manny explains that he is going to eat her and lick each letter of the alphabet across her vulva. She has to guess which letter he is licking and call it out. If she can recite to "Z," Manny loses and can't make love to her.

Manny starts with the letter "A."

Several hours later Manny awakes with Felicia lying next to him. He has a big smile on his face.

Manny spends the night at the restaurant. Lena starts to suspect what is going on but keeps quiet. Lena has mixed feelings about what her role should be. Her emotions get the better of her. The next day as Manny gets home, he intercepts the mail that is going to Lena and brings it up to her.

MANNY: "Honey, there's an envelope for you."

Lena finds the photo of Felicia and flips out. Manny's only defense is to say that Felicia is stalking him and that he was unaware of her infatuation. His problems with Felicia seem to get worse. Several weeks later, Felicia tells Manny she is pregnant. Manny is unaware that there are forces that are working against Felicia that are beyond anyone's control due to a spell by Dominica, thinking Felicia is Lena. Felicia has a miscarriage and winds up in intensive care.

Manny tries to make it work with Lena. She also falls under the same spell and had two miscarriages. Her hospital stay seems to drag on. Manny can't seem to figure out why her recovery is taking so long. Dominica has put a powerful spell against any woman who would keep her daughter from Manny. She will do absolutely anything to keep Manny with Carmen.

SEVERAL DAYS LATER

Lena has come home from the hospital and is recovering from her ordeal. The doctor tells them that with proper healing and recovery, they could try again at some future time. Manny tells Lena not to worry, that he sees a family in their future. He assures her that their luck is about to change. Manny's cell phone rings at that moment. He hesitates and then picks up.

LENA: "What's wrong, Manny?"

MANNY: "It's Carmen!"

LENA: "Something happened to Carmen?"

MANNY: "No, Carmen is okay."

MANNY: "Her mother, Dominica, was found at the bottom of the stairs with her neck broken."

CHAPTER FOUR

THE TWO FACES OF LOVE

This was my fifth and probably her tenth orgasm. She didn't seem to mind that the sheets were soaking in our sweat and the bed reeked of sex. The more I pushed in to her, the more she grabbed at the bedpost and screamed.

DIANA: "That's all you got? Come on, Al, f**k me harder! What's the matter, baby? Are you running out of milk? F**k me harder!"

The more she screams these words, the harder I push into her. This was the type of woman I loved. Two hours in this position were making my knees numb. I motion to her that I needed to pull out.

DIANA: "You better not pull out, you bastard! I'm almost there!"

FADE TO FULL STORY

My name is Al. I work in the maintenance department at Georgian College. I've been divorced for over five years and just recently started dating again. At first I was shy about the whole dating scene. Getting back into dating after a failed marriage is not easy. Then I started a new job two years ago at the school. This is when everything started to change for me. My job at the school gives me the luxury of meeting all kinds of women. White, black, brown, it doesn't matter—I've had them all and continue to have them. I'm Polish and I have an accent that drives zee ladies crazy. I pulled off a lot of panties, and most of the women I went out with had a lot in common. Then I met Diana.

I first met Diana at a trendy bar in Manhattan. She had this air about her that drew me to her. She was a real looker. Her walk was nothing less than spectacular. When she walked, all men stopped what they were doing to look at her. There was something about her that almost seemed too good to be true. She asked the bartender to send me a drink on her tab. After accepting my gift, I hesitated for a few minutes. While we shared stares of interest, my hormones took over as I glided over toward her seat.

AL: "Hi, thanks for the drink. My name is Albert, and you are…?"

DIANA: "I'm Diana. It looked like you needed a drink."

AL: "Thank you."

DIANA: "My pleasure."

ALBERT: "What are you, psychic?"

DIANA: "Not even close, but a good guesser. What are you, a guard?"

ALBERT: "I work in maintenance at Georgian College. And you?"

DIANA: "I work for an insurance company in midtown."

We talked and shared our interests and found that we had a lot in common. I walked Diana home and arranged to have another night out. This would be the beginning of many nights out.

On our third date, the night ended with heavy rain that caught us by surprise. Diana invited me up to her apartment to dry off. She took my clothes and offered me a towel. While the clothes were tumbling in the dryer, we had a few drinks. We found ourselves on her couch sharing our saliva and exploring each other's bodies with our hands. Diana seems to take great pleasure in the art of foreplay. Her hands seem to relish every part of my body that she touched.

To Diana it wasn't the final act of intercourse that excited her the most; the excitement for her was the tease leading to intercourse. This was one of the things that made her different. She grabbed my penis and played with me till her hands were soaked with fluid and took pleasure in teasing me close to ejaculation. Every time I came close, she would pull back and start over. You could see the excitement on her face.

This hot blonde teased cum out of me by dressing in erotic lingerie. Her arsenal of erotica includes crotchless pantyhose, micro miniskirts, and high heels. Diana loves to tease me as well as please me by dressing in sexy outfits.

With Diana it was different because she never chased me or called me first. She always waited for me to call her. This was something that I wasn't used to. I never chased a woman in my life, and here I found myself being drawn to her. I get twenty calls on my cell phone. No call back from her 'til midweek. When we did get together at her place, she paraded around with her crotchless fishnet body stocking. This type of erotica was new and exciting to me.

On one of our nights out, I noticed that Diana took a bottle out and popped a few pills. When I asked her about this, she told me that she was taking some medication for an allergic condition. I accepted that reason and never gave it another thought. This would later come back to haunt me in its own way.

Diana, like myself, loved clothes and we found ourselves shopping in a lot of high-end stores. She was almost fanatical about how her clothes had to fit. I brought Diana out to a lot of fine restaurants around the city and introduced her to my friends and roommates. On one such occasion my roommate Bernie said that Diana looked very familiar, but he couldn't remember where he'd seen her.

The guys that I live with, Bernie and Victor, think I'm losing it. They said they've never seen me act the way I was with Diana. Bernie asks me if I knew anything about Diana's past. Because he worked as a private investigator, he offered to look into her background. I told him that he was being foolish again. He had an annoying habit of investigating everyone he met.

Things were getting pretty serious between Diana and me. We'd been going out for over a year and a half .She gave me hints about making a commitment and living together. For the first time I was actually giving it serious thought. My bond with her was such that I needed to see or hear from her at least three times a day.

Because of these feelings, I decided to seek the advice of a psychic. I needed to know where my future was with Diana. Through a mutual friend I sought the help of a psychic known as Psychic Cindy. She was very well known and at the top of her field. Cindy advised me to be careful. She saw a woman walking into my life, but wasn't sure if Diana was the one. Psychic Cindy said she saw a man coming between Diana and myself, but wasn't clear who that was.

Unknown to Al, his friend Bernie begins some investigation work on Diana. Bernie ran online background checks on her, but kept coming up with blanks. Diana had no background to be found. She was a mystery woman. She had no history of birth and no history of family. Bernie decided to make use of his surveillance equipment and follow her. Al was like a brother to him, and there was something that didn't feel right about this woman.

During one of his surveillances, Bernie follows Diana to a building down near the SoHo section of Manhattan. She spends a little over a two hours, and then leaves to go to a local nail salon near her home.

Meanwhile Al has been thinking about popping the big question to Diana. He goes shopping near the Manhattan diamond district comparing prices on diamond rings. He enters a store on Forty-eighth Street and Sixth Avenue.

DIAMOND SALESMAN "Yes, sir, can I help you?"

ALBERT: "Hello, I'm looking for an engagement ring in the two-carat size range."

DIAMOND SALESMAN "Sure, sir, I can help you with that. When do you need this by?"

ALBERT: "It needs to be ready in about three weeks."

DIAMOND SALESMAN: "No problem. Right this way. Let me show you what we have in that range."

Bernie is not having any luck with solving the mystery of Diana's background. He decides to pay a visit to the place where she goes to every Tuesday and Thursday in SoHo. When he gets there, he sees a sign on the door that says, "BY APPOINTMENT ONLY." Bernie knocks on the door. A short gentleman in a white overcoat opens the door.

DOCTOR LEVINE: "Can I help you?"

As Bernie speaks he looks over his shoulder, scanning the inside of the office, and sees only a simple desk and chair and a door to another room.

BERNIE: "Yes, I was looking for a lady, blonde hair, about five foot eight?"

Doctor Levine has a smile on his face.

DOCTOR LEVINE: "You and about four hundred other men. Just teasing you! You mean Diana?"

BERNIE: "Yes, could you tell me why she was here?"

DOCTOR LEVINE: "That I cannot do. It's doctor-patient confidentiality."

BERNIE: "Look, a friend of mine is going out with this woman."

DOCTOR LEVINE "Please! I've heard it all before."

BERNIE: "Can you help me out here, doc?"

DOCTOR LEVINE: "Not a fat chance, buddy! Look, you seem to be a nice guy, but I really can't give that kind of information out. What kind of reputation do you think I would have if I spilled my guts to every jerk who walks through that door? What are you trying to do—put me out of business?"

BERNIE: "Thanks for nuttin', doc. You're a real lifesaver."

FADE TO SCENE WITH ALBERT AT CUCHIFRITOS'S RESTAURANT

Al has made arrangements at one of his favorite restaurants for him and Diana.

When the ring moment comes, a woman and two guys will come to their table to sing "Our Day Will Come." Bernie's next move is to get a fingerprint and have it processed through the bureau for ID.

Parked outside Diana's apartment, he waits for her to come out of her building. Like clockwork, she exits her building on her way to work. As she walks down the subway entrance, Bernie exits his car and heads toward her building.

He jimmies the lock and enters the apartment and locks the door behind him. As he scans her apartment for any sign of history, Diana realizes she's forgotten her building entrance ID. She turns around and heads back to her apartment. Bernie enters the kitchen and finds a half-full glass with a perfect print on it. He empties the glass and places it inside a plastic bag. At that moment he hears someone fidgeting at the door. Bernie heads to the bedroom closet and quickly closes the door behind him. He leaves it open just enough to get a partial view of the room.

Diana comes in and heads to her bedroom where her ID is lying on the bureau. She quickly pockets it and heads for the door. She pauses for a few seconds and looks toward the kitchen, where the glass is now missing. She looks in that direction, shakes her head, then continues out the door.

Bernie waits for a few minutes, comes out of the closet quietly, and moves the window curtains gently over while peeping out. He sees Diana headed back toward the subway. As Bernie heads out the door, he notices a bottle of pills that he didn't see before. He pockets it and in five minutes Bernie is in his car headed for the lab with his glass and pills. It takes about a week to process the print that was retrieved from the glass at Diana's place. The label on the bottle was taken off, so the lab has to do an analysis to determine what the medication is.

Unaware of Bernie's extra activities, Al tells Bernie and Victor of his plans for the engagement party. The boys are excited, but no one is more nervous than Bernie.

Al and Diana are dining at The West Shore, where they are met by friends and associates of Al. The ring was picked up earlier that day, and Al has it in one of the safes at the college. While Al prepares for the engagement celebration, Bernie has just received identification from the print taken off the glass and lab results from the drugs found at Diana's apartment.

As Bernie comes to grips with what he reads, he gets in his car and quickly heads for the restaurant. Barely missing some cars along the way, Bernie hopes that it is not too late.

As his car screeches and bumps the sidewalk, Bernie rushes out of his vehicle. He charges to the restaurant's front entrance. Restaurant security intercepts him, thinking he is someone else, and he struggles with them.

BERNIE: "Let go of me, you idiot! I'm Bernie! I need to speak to Albert immediately."

SECURITY: "Stay right where you are for a second!"

BERNIE: "Man, what's wrong with you? I'm Al's roommate! What the f**k is your problem?"

As security restrains Bernie, they get on the radio.

SECURITY: "Yes, this is security. We have a gentleman named Bernie, says he needs to see Al ASAP. Know this guy?"

Unable to wait, Bernie attempts to push his way through but is held back by security.

Al, noticing that there is a scuffle at the door, gets up and sees Bernie fighting with security.

Al immediately heads to the front door.

He yells out, "It's okay, I know him!" Bernie rushes to Al and, catching his breath, yells, "She's a he!!! Diana's real name is David Rhodes. He had a sex change surgery three years ago in England. I did a background check on her prints. I found female hormone pills in her apartment. I swear to God it's true! I swear to God! I even have before pictures, to prove it."

Shocked by the news, Al stands there paralyzed with his mouth wide open. In the background a waiter has arrived at his table with the engagement ring neatly packaged.

Unaware of what's happening up front, Diana waits at the table with a smile on her face as she looks to the ring-size box brought by the waiter………

GQ The Man

Fade from low volume to mid volume
Song "Love to Love You Baby" by Donna Summers

While Vicky was giving me oral, I was eating Rachel out. We were placing hundred-dollar bets on who would last longer, me or Rachel? What the girls didn't know was I popped a couple of stay-hard pills. I was going to last the night. This was one of my secret methods of keeping the ladies coming back to me.

The boys had given me the ultimate bachelor's birthday gift. I wasn't about to disappoint them. I also never lose a bet. I called this threesome the GQ Stallion, because you have to be a stallion to win this bet without the pills.

FADE TO FULL STORY

My name is GQ.

My roommates call me that because of the way I dress. I love to dress in eight-hundred-dollar suits. There is nothing that I wouldn't do to try to get the finest suit or trendy shoes. I'm also known as GQ because I love myself most of all.

Seven years ago I arrived in the United States from Italy with nothing but my good looks and a bag of clothes. I quickly learned that in order to succeed in America, you have to work very hard at it. My goal is to one day own my own restaurant.

My second love is restaurant management. My expertise is in restaurant marketing. Owners of restaurants know that I'll make their restaurant profitable. It's not only about money. I bring their restaurant out in the open and get them in culinary magazines. My job is simply to make restaurants famous establishments.

The allure of the restaurant business to me was like no other. It is one of the most exciting industries around. I'm Italian with the ability to speak fluent Spanish. This gives me the biggest edge among my colleagues. I can speak to two of the hottest women around: Latinas and Italian women. Among other things I can cook Spanish as well as Italian cuisine. Due to my restaurant business, I have to have two separate cell phones. One cell phone is for business and one for pleasure.

I do very well with my restaurant business, so I live in a mansion with two older bachelors, Donator and Vito. My business attracts a lot of women, and I take full advantage of that. My roommates make fun of me because of the many women who are always knocking on our door. One of these women was a girl named Ginger.

Ginger likes to tease you to death before she allows you to touch her. She was all about the tease. I met Ginger when I was at the Metro bank. She was on the line in front of me. About two minutes after I walked in, she kept looking back at me. She was a redhead about five feet nine, slender. She wore a tight black skirt with classic spectator pumps. Her open-buttoned red blouse looked like it was painted on her. I finally had to say something. It would be unlike GQ to say nothing!

GQ: "Is there something that I can help you with?"

GINGER: "I was just wondering if I knew you, because you look familiar. Where have I seen you before?"

GQ: "Well, I do a lot of work in restaurants in the city."

GINGER: "Maybe. Anyway, what's your name?"

GQ: "My name is GQ. And yours?"

GINGER: "GQ. Hmm, it fits you. My name is Ginger. I work at the city morgue. When I say that, it usually ends the conversation."

GQ: "Well, you have to make a living, right?"

GINGER: "Hey, that's funny!! Make a living. You're pretty cute. You're not married, right?"

GQ: "That's a good guess! How did you know?"

GINGER: "I don't know. The way you dress. Married guys don't dress like you. You dress like you're hunting for something."

GQ: "Hunting?"

GINGER: "You know what I mean."

GQ pauses then says, "No."

GINGER: "You dress like you give a sh*t."

GQ: "Maybe. Maybe I already found my prey."

When Ginger hears that line, her left eye starts to twitch. GQ catches that movement and goes in for the kill.

GQ: "Would you like to have lunch or dinner sometime?"

GINGER: "Okay, that sounds nice."

GQ: "Do you have a number where I can squeeze, ah, I mean, reach you?"

GINGER: "Here's my cell number. I'm home after six p.m. mostly. But you can 'squeeze' me anytime, silly."

That night as I headed home, I wondered if she would even answer the call. She intrigued me with her hunting questions. Ginger lived up near Sixty-Sixth Street, near the FDR Drive.

It was a pretty well-kept yuppie-type building. When I arrived to pick her up, she greeted me at the door in a strapless floral corset. Before I could say anything she interrupted me.

GINGER: "I was thinking if it's all right with you, we could eat in."

GQ: "I love eating. Uh, I mean, I enjoy eating in."

While she paraded around in her corset, I was trying to hide my excitement. The truth was that I was as hard as a rock and getting harder. It had been a while since I'd seen a corset, and this one had a thong panty. Ginger also had a body that would wake up even the dead. Six drinks later, I had Ginger in my arms and we were locked lips to lips. I could feel her private rubbing against my boner as we heated up our bodies with each movement.

Ginger removed her panty and rubbed it on my nose as if to mark her property. The scent sent sexual electricity through my body, by signaling my mind to think imminent copulation. I immediately grow harder and bigger.

Soundtrack: "Stronger" by Kanye West

The outcome that is playing in my mind is confirmed by each move that Ginger makes.

As she removes her corset, my right leg starts shaking the "I'm going to have sex" shake.

GINGER: "Why are you shaking so much, baby?"

GQ: "Just nerves. Don't happen all the time, just every so often."

GINGER: "Don't worry, baby. No need to be nervous with me. Are you nice and wet?"

101

Just as I was ready to answer, Ginger jumped on top of me with great force.

GINGER: "Oops, I forgot to tell you, I like to be dry when you enter me. I want to feel your skin, baby. I like it rough!!! I like it raw, baby! Nice daddy!"

FADE TO OTHER SCENE

Talia stood out like an orchid stands out among wildflowers. She had not only an outward beauty but carried with her an inward beauty as well. We met at one of my restaurants that I was promoting. She was sitting alone as I was consulting with the owner, Mr. Ramos, about the ambiance of the restaurant. I found out later on that Russian women take care of their bodies and actually enjoy looking pretty.

The GQ radar was going off, and I was finding it increasingly difficult to concentrate on business and ignore this Russian beauty. I excused myself for a moment and approached Major, a good colleague of mine.

GQ: "See that lady in the blue dress at table seven?"

MAJOR: "Shit, yeah, been checking her out all evening."

GQ: "Who is she?"

MAJOR: "Yo man, her name is Talia. Some Russian babe I think. She is so hot; I can feel the heat from here."

GQ: "I got to meet her. Do me a favor. Give me about three minutes and tell the owner there are a couple of strange guys looking at his car."

GQ slips a Benjamin into Major's hand and walks back to the business owner. GQ knows that there is no way that Mr. Ramos is going to take a chance on his Porsche. That should buy him about ten minutes. GQ the lady man will have this woman's number in his wallet by the time the owner gets back to him.

Three minutes later the owner is on his way to the parking area to check on his car.

GQ walks over to Talia's table, smoothing down his hair and centering his tie on his Double-breasted Armani suit.

GQ: "Excuse me; I'm with the restaurant customer service. Just want to make sure everything is all right with our service."

TALIA: "Oh, how nice of you to ask. I was just admiring your restaurants here in America. Are all of them as beautiful as this one?"

GQ: "Only the ones that I take care of."

Talia gives a delayed laugh at his remark.

GQ: "Are you from out of state?"

TALIA: "I am here from Russian university on limited visit visa."

GQ: "My name is GQ. Your English is very good. How long have you been here?"

TALIA: "Thank you; my name is Natalia. But everyone calls me Talia. I'm only three weeks. Learned English at University Lomonsov. In about four weeks I go back to Russia."

GQ: "Would you like to go to a real American party while you're here?"

TALIA: "Okay, sounds like fun. I'm staying at the Drake Hotel, Room 202. Here's the number."

GQ: "Great! I'll call you about 7 p.m. Enjoy your meal."

By the time I left Talia's table, Mr. Ramos was walking back into the restaurant's dining area.

FIVE HOURS LATER AT TALIA'S HOTEL ROOM

Talia senses that I didn't like being tied up, but her game was so out of control I couldn't help but play along with her. This thirty-two-year-old brunette beauty was going to have her way with me. She tied my hands behind my back and bound my ankles together. She placed me with my face down on her bed. She then spread-eagled with her legs apart and her crotch in front of my face.

Talia's rule was to keep me tied until I followed her every command with my tongue. We took turns and then I would bind her up and switch places. She called this game "trading places." Talia had a knack for making a man feel great. I was Excited, but yet a little taken back; no woman has been able to ever capture the heart of GQ - that's just not possible. I just noticed I am thinking about this woman a little too much.

FADE TO NEXT SCENE

While walking Talia home one evening, I noticed two guys standing in front of her building one was smoking the other on the cell phone yelling in Russian while we approached the building. Talia with excitement yelled Roman! Genya what are you guys doing here? When did you get here? Omg! GQ, these are my brothers. Oh my, how is momma? Ok let's go upstairs. Where are you staying? Did you find something? Stay with me the night.

GQ: "Do you want me to leave so you can spend time with your brothers?"

TALIA: "Why? I want them to meet you."

GQ: "I mean tomorrow is another day how about bring them to the restaurant at 8:00pm."

TALIA: "Ok my love, see you tomorrow."

GQ: "I'm going. Ciao."

FROM GQ'S MIND

After leaving Talia's place, I was so excited to meet her brother's. Wow! That had never happened before. I have to go home and speak with the guys.

I got home, poured me a Remy martin. In came Donato.

GQ: "Yo bro, come have a drink with me. I need to talk."

My feelings for Talia were starting to grow deeper than ever. A confused feeling was coming over me.

DONATO: "I don't know this is not the GQ man."

GQ: "I love all kinds of woman. I am not calling anyone back. I don't know what to do? "

DONATO: "Sounds like your falling in love!"

GQ: "NAH! Are you kidding No, absolutely not?"

I have to think about this. I know, tomorrow I decided to seek the advice of a personal friend; Psychic Cindy.

PSYCHIC CINDY: "Hi, how are you? It's been a while GQ. How are the ladies lol"

GQ: "OMG! You have no idea I need the cards. Let's pull them"

PSYCHIC CINDY: "Well you have done a lot in just a few months I'm happy for you."

PSYCHIC CINDY: "But there is something different about you? Mmmmm, I see a huge change about you today. Well, March is definitely the month for you - New Beginning's - a the female that is in is definitely different from any other.."

PSYCHIC CINDY: "Feelings is a new challenge for you."

GQ: "What do you mean by that?"

PSYCHIC CINDY: "You have very strong feelings for this girl?"

GQ: "Well, yes, I do, Cindy!"

PSYCHIC CINDY: "This is a switch. Your insides are filled with butterflies; your thoughts are all occupied of her every day and every minute BUT!"

PSYCHIC CINDY: "How do you know this girl is who she says she is? I see her with 2 faces. That's not a good sign, I don't have good feelings. There is a secret that's coming out, sooner than you think! Hold on to your heart, don't share it too much with her, be careful, my friend. Unknown waters run deep! I want you to carry this prayer card of St Michael. He will protect you against the evil that's lurks up on you. Betrayal's all around you."

GQ: "Me, pray? I never pray."

PSYCHIC CINDY: "Remember, keep this card in your wallet and say the prayer once a day! St Michael hears you."

GQ: "I couldn't help wondering why I was falling deeply for this creature of beauty."

BACK AT TALIA'S APARTMENT

Behind closed doors Talia takes her panties off, dips them in a glass of fresh water, squeezes a little lemon in it, puts it in the fridge—that's her secret remedy for her to land her GQ man. This is done three times a week. Talia is doing very hard spells to land GQ.

Everything was going smoothly with Talia. She had GQ in her hands calling her, showering her with gifts, wanting to stay at her place, enjoying the visit with her brothers.

I was on cloud nine. No one could absolutely crush me; the feelings I have inside are unexplainable and couldn't control. I got rid of my little black book, shut my cell down to the woman of society and re-opened one just for us and my business.

Until one day I decided to visit Talia about an hour earlier than promised. Upon arriving, I noticed Roman's car that he rented outside Talia's building.

I looked up at her apartment window and saw him through the curtains. That was ok, but I wanted to spend time with Talia. As great as it was, I was getting tired of the brothers always around. I can't wait for them to go back. As I approach the door, I hear music playing. I knock on the door. No one answer's so I turn the knob and open the door.

GQ: "What the hell?!"

"What the hell is going on here?"

Genya had his head so deep in Talia's private eating her out all you saw was his shoulders. I look up and see Talia was giving oral to Roman on the floor like a wild orgy party! There wasn't any resistance from Talia. I could not believe what my eyes were seeing, All my emotions were running wild, at the same time my left eye for the first time started to twitch. I grab Genya, punched him in the face while Roman quickly grab his pants jumped me from behind. Talia is screaming;

TALIA: "Wait! You don't understand. Please stop Roman! Don't hurt him! Genya, wait, stop!"

As the brothers have me pinned on the floor, punching me, kicking me, my mouth is bleeding. I can't see out of my right eyeball I can hear Talia crying and yelling for them to stop. I observe Roman getting his clothes on, grabs Talia's arm and starts tonguing her while saying, "take care of this, I'll call you later." Roman slaps Talia on the ass and walks out.

Genya spits on me and kicks me again on my side then slams the door. Talia rushes over to me with this look in her eyes. I think this is the first time in 5 months I actually saw some emotion from her that was honest but also the worst of her. Talia leans over but has never seen anyone look at her the way GQ did. It was more than disgust or even shame. It was like his eyes as beautiful as they are, they were dead eyes. As Talia gets GQ up on his feet to the couch, he pulls away from her and heads toward the door holding his side and walking very slow from the pain he feels. He opens the door, he looks back at her shaking his head and lets out a little laugh to himself and leaves.

FROM THE MIND OF GQ:

GQ gets in his car and sits there for a few. He can't even phantom what has happened. He is going over and over in his head what just happened. He is in shock! GQ drives off with no destination in mind and finds himself in Brooklyn at the promenade he always feels peaceful. Over here, especially at night, the moon is out, the weather is 78 degrees. People are walking, but yet minding their own business. As I walk over to the bench, an older lady that sitting there moves over so I can sit. A few seconds later, without saying a word, she hands me a white handkerchief to clean my lip up from the blood that was oozing out and walked away.

I thought to myself while having a Heineken. Why? How? How the hell did this happen and why? What the hell happened to me? How could I not see and how sick no a nightmare this is. I am now starting to feel rage. I cannot help myself; she was f*$king me and her brothers. How sick is that? God only knows I am praying and yelling at God at the same time, My Heart is not only ripped out; I am a total mess as any one person can be.

I want to die. Even worse, I cannot talk to anyone about this because I am humiliated! That I, GQ, was taken by this bitch! Was this my punishment for the way I have treated all women who have loved me and I treated not so right? God, please hear me; hear my prayers. I need answers. As I look over the railing on the promenade I can see cars underneath heading to the BQE. I see the ocean with the ships docked ahead. The tears running down my face I cannot wipe them away fast enough. I decide I have to go and see Psychic Cindy. I call her and I get the answering machine No! No! No!

I decide to drive to her home. I see her lights on and ring the bell. Cindy answers the door, sees me, grabs and hugs me. Her embracing me feels so good at that moment. I buckle and start crying even more. I have never felt a woman hold me the way she did at that moment.

PSYCHIC CINDY: "I knew you would come. I am so sorry. Look at you. Come, let me clean you up and give you some hot herbal tea."

GQ: "You warned me. I am so sorry I did not believe you. I thought, I don't know what I thought, but I never felt like this before. Cindy can you understand that?"

PSYCHIC CINDY: "Yes I can. It will be a while but you will be ok. I will be right by your side. Love is an emotion that hurts and makes you feel good; it's up and down. That's how you know it's real."

GQ: "Cindy she was sleeping with her brothers. She used me for money to send back to her family. The brothers came down because it was 2 months and they got nothing so they were checking up on Talia. She is a good con artist. I just feel sick to my stomach of that scene. You don't understand what it's like to see her brothers and her at that moment. No one can truly know. I kept thinking, why? Why me?"

PSYCHIC CINDY: "Have a little Tea with me and we'll talk"

GQ: "Okay. Ouch that's hot"

PSYCHIC CINDY: "A little sip is good for you. Trust me."

GQ: "Wiping the tears that are still flooding down his face?"

Cindy looked at me and seemed to be thinking about my words. She looks a little scared. She obviously is feeling something from me.

After 2 hours of being with Cindy I still did not feel any better. I just wanted to crawl in a hole and die! Psychic Cindy had me take one of her special Baths and gave me 2 more to take at home.

I headed home and stayed in darkness for 2 weeks. My roommates were crazed with fear that I might do something. They have never seen me this way and could not understand. I refused to listen and my appearance started taken on the look of a man on the wagon. I slept in the same clothes I wore throughout the day. My beard was filling in fast due to lack of shaving.

I decided today, Tuesday, was going to be a beginning for me. My boss was almost practically at my door everyday now; everything in my life was in jeopardy. I have to get my life not only back, but in order. I got up, took a shower, used one of the special baths, shaved and finally went to work. I was missing in action for several weeks. I went to work and I see one of the girls reading a book called "The Desire to Love."

I just pass by like nothing, but yet it peak my curiosity. I continued with my day; it felt good to be back. My coworkers noticed something different in me. Miriam the waitress had suggested the book "The Law of Attraction" to me. That this will put my mind in a better place. I looked at her like what? Does she know? And how? OMG! It's now five months later and I'm on top of the world! My scars are not visible, but they are still there. I started to limit myself to just one woman. I felt God had indeed punished me. I met Sieria, a beautiful slim brunette. She is very hard working and passionate about family values. We are on a good path, and I like the fact that now I am starting to want to settle down. My thoughts are now about having a family. I know that what happened to me will stay with me for life. It's not something that goes away overnight. Talia used me but now that is in the past. I've accepted the reality that incest does exist. I wonder how and why people do what they do. As Psychic Cindy would say, sometimes in life there are no answers, my love. I finally moved out and got my own place. I felt it was time to hang up the bachelor pad and start taking life serious for once. It's been nine months now. I haven't seen the guys that much and miss them so tonight were catching up. I hear Donato has a chick that might be the one. I'm glad for him.

EPILOGUE

Donato and Vito are very happy to see me when I arrived.

DONATO: "Where have you been hiding, Mr. GQ?"

VITO: "Yeah, where ya been? I miss you guy."

GQ: "Getting my life back in order but in a healthy way!"

DONATO: "I bet you have. What's her name?"

GQ: "You're so funny; you don't understand. My life changed completely since, well you know, that I don't even want to get into it. Something died inside me, but yet something grew, if you can understand that."

VITO: "She was a pig? If I see her I would spit on her and the brothers."

GQ: "I don't want to talk about it. We're here; come here let me hug you guys. I miss you."
"Raise your drink salute! To us I love ya."

DONATO: "This damn phone never stops ringing. Hold one sec. Hey baby, what's going on? Where are you?"
No I'm at Che Che's place with the guys. Come by, I want you to meet them."

GQ: "Who's that on the phone?"

DONATO: "Veronica. You have got to see her .This is the one bro, you don't understand she takes care of me, fusses over me. A guy can't get it any better. Her family is coming in next week were going to have a get together."

GQ: "Wow! I'm happy for you Donato you deserve it so. Vito, what about you?"

VITO: "Well, Sue and I are looking for a place we are expecting our first! It's a boy! And Donato is asking Veronica to marry him. All is good."

DONATO: "I just bought a 30 foot yacht and was going to take her and her family out next week. Come with Sieria and join us GQ."
We would love to meet this woman who has finally got the GQ Man to settle down."

GQ: "Oh, we'll see."

DONATO: "Oh. Here she is now! Veronica, over here baby."

In comes this woman smelling like a fragrance of passion flowers. As GQ starts to turn around and get up to meet Veronica, their eyes meet and with fear GQ starts screaming;

"Talia! You Bitch!"

GQ starts choking her, knocking her to the floor, screaming

"I'll kill you bitch..........You ruined my life...ahhhhhhh I'll kill you.............."

END OF SCENE

G-SPOT

OPENING SCENE

Its 3 a.m. on level three of the tri-state hospital parking area. A nurse and doctor are inside a vehicle with steamy windows.

BARBARA: "S#it! Be careful, Herps. This is the third time you ripped my pantyhose. Why can't you be gentler? Can't you wait? My p#@% isn't going anywhere."

HERPS: "I'm sorry, Barbara. I've been thinking about you all day. Every time I bumped into you and saw that booty popping up. Can't help myself!"

The tear that Herps had formed in Barbara's pantyhose wasn't an accident. He ripped a hole in the crotch area big enough for him to enter her vagina without removing the hose. This was becoming a turn-on for him. With the passenger seat folded all the way back, Barbara's left foot kept hitting the horn. Her right foot laid just outside the passenger window as Herps pumped his way to an inevitable orgasm.

HERPS: "Stop hitting the horn."

BARBARA: "What horn?"

HERPS: "The freaking horn next to your foot. Someone is going to hear us."

FADE TO FULL STORY

My name is Barbara. I'm black, thirty-two years old, and I absolutely love white men. I will date Latin men as well. I love a man who has blond hair and blue eyes. I'm especially fond of men who are well hung. My goal is to achieve the ultimate orgasm. I not only want to get off, but I want to get off big-time. They say that the ultimate orgasm for a woman can induce her to a comatose state or death. I'm willing to take that chance. Most of the guys I date never seem to be able to find my G-spot, let alone know what it is. When this happens, I just know that it's going to be a long night. That reminds me of the man I buy bootleg DVDs from. He is definitely a negative zero when it comes to sex. Jim always tells me how much he loves me. He tells me one day I'll marry him and no one else. At least I get some decent DVDs from him. It seems to be about the only thing decent he has.

JR is a guy who lives on the fifth floor in the same building as me. I live on the third floor. JR comes down Tuesdays and Thursdays after I watch my CSI shows. I have great sex with JR all night. He's my young midnight Latin snack. He's a big-time player who is muscle bound, about five-feet-five, with a trim mustache and receding hairline.

Being a nurse as my cover, I had the benefit of observing all types of male bodies. Beyond the obvious differences in the size of males' sex organ, the little head always screws over the big head.

At night I work for a private investigation firm. My nick name is G-spot. Years ago when I was in my early twenties, I discovered that I had the ability to influence almost any man sexually instantaneously. This ability goes beyond the natural flirt and tease. I discovered quite by accident that I could cause a man to submit to me regardless of his desire or not. I can put a man into a trance as long as I make eye contact. Two years ago, a crazed man was holding a knife at a one-year-old boy during a domestic dispute. I was just passing by and I looked at the man directly into his eyes. For the sake of that child, I asked him to drop the knife. Once I made eye contact with my sexual thoughts concentrated on him, he released the knife. The officer at the scene was able to separate him from the child and take him into custody.

My partner I work with is known as DT Chief Tenafly. Tenafly works well with me and understands my abilities. We work for a special investigative unit of the investigation firm. Tenafly called me in about a case he was working on for three months over in New Jersey. He tells me it is a bias-type crime and could potentially get out of control.

DT TANAFLY: "I need your help on this one, G. This is the third one this week. The Hasidic community is putting pressure on the mayor. The mayor is putting pressure on the governor." Victim was a female Hasidic in her early twenties. The victim had been raped and had a swastika symbol scrawled on her chest."

When I got to the crime scene, the lab crew had not arrived yet. That meant the crime scene was still fresh.

The body was face up with her right leg bent at the knee, spread to the side. Her left leg stretched over to the far left, almost in a 45-degree angle. Her left calf was bent behind her to her left; with the heel pointing up. Whoever did this was very strong. There was a lot of anger behind this rape. The victim had a bruise on her cheek and forehead. Blood was gushing out her mouth. She had been struck, possibly to avoid fighting back or to quiet her. Her neck had the mark of fingers imbedded in her skin. There were bruises on her inner thigh but no sign of semen. Her hands were bound behind her with a cord.

The black, ankle-length skirt she was wearing had been torn off her body and tossed several feet away. Her panties were also ripped off but are missing. The mark of the panty line was left on her waist. There was a piece of her torn pink panties that I recovered from the scene. I placed it in a plastic bag and pocketed it. I found her purse behind a bush. After putting on vinyl gloves, I was able to retrieve an ID from her license. The lab boys were just arriving when I was finishing up my visual inspection.

LAB TECH JIM: "What's up, G?"

G-SPOT: "Twenty-three-year-old female Chaya Millers appears to be a victim of rape. Just like the other three."

LAB TECH JIM: "Find anything unusual?"

G-SPOT: "Nope. Other than missing panties like the other two."

LAB TECH DAVID: "Are you kidding me?"

LAB TECH JIM: "God, man, a panty collector."

LAB TECH DAVID: "I hate the weird ones."

G-SPOT: "I was waiting for you to have first pickings."

LAB TECH DAVID: "Sure, I bet you were. This is perfect for you, anyway. It looks to be fetish to me."

David was right. This wasn't just a bias crime; it was mixed with some fetish. I knew that the lab guys were good at what they did. They did not have the experience with crimes that lean on the freaky side. That was my specialty. It would be some time before the lab results from the crime scene were in. It was Friday night, and I had a date with John, my mechanic.

When my doorbell rang, I was just stepping out of the shower. I reached for a towel and wrapped it around my waist, barely covering my breast. I knew it was John and wanted to give him a glimpse of paradise.

As I headed for the door, I walked into my bedroom, put my slippers on quickly. When I opened the door, he stood there like a Trojan warrior ready to do battle. John had on black nylon pants that hugged his muscular body like a leather glove. His chest stuck out from the open gold short-sleeve shirt like it had permission. All I kept staring at was the bulge at his crotch.

G-Spot: "Hi, John. Come in, grab a seat. I'll be with you in a moment, just getting out of the shower."

As I turned around ,I bent over to pick up a slipper that came off my foot as I went for the door. I reached down and bent over, exposing my butt and private. I knew he was looking and it sent a rushed through my body. As I replaced my slipper, I pretended to lose my footing and dropped my towel. I quickly retrieved it and excused myself before disappearing into my bedroom. I yelled from my room, "It isn't like you haven't seen me naked before, right? What's the matter? Why are you so quiet tonight?"

John: "Come on now, quit teasing. I don't want us to be late."

John was so quiet at the restaurant. I knew it was the calm before the storm. I also knew he enjoyed me teasing him. A storm was brewing inside him and it was a Category 5.

While we were talking, I slipped out of my right heel and slowly worked my right leg up alongside John's crotch area. The tablecloth covered the scene. It was fun to see John's face change from his smile to one of awkward sexual excitement. I worked my toe alongside John's crotch and rubbed him from tip to base in a slow, rhythmic motion. I could feel his member grow and get harder as I continued to rub.

G-Spot: "How was your steak, John?"

John: "Steak—what steak? Oh yeah, it's good, hard, uh, I mean soft, just the way I like it. Is your meal okay?"

G-Spot: "Yep, not really too hungry for food right now. I'm hungry for that other meat, baby."

John: "You know, if you keep rubbing me, I won't be able to stand up."

G-Spot: "Why?"

John: "You know why. Stop it now!! You're going to raise the Titanic. Besides, we got plenty of time for that. Damn, now I have a stain! Shit! I need a towel to keep in front of me!"

When we got back to John's place, he got even for my restaurant behavior. He ripped my thong off and rode me like he had a gun to his head.

G-Spot: "John, goddammit, slow down, slow down."

With Barbara spread out looking like an upside down T, John pumped his way to an eventual orgasm.

FADE TO OTHER SCENE

On a tree-lined suburban street in New Jersey, an Orthodox-looking woman walks down the avenue at 7 p.m. in the evening. She is being monitored by several unmarked cars several blocks away. This is her ninth time around the area. Over her hearing piece she hears,

Dt Benny: "Okay, Lucy, let's call it a night. He must have gotten spooked."

Dt Lucy Riviera: "He's got to be here; can't we give it another try?"

Dt Joe: "If he was, he's gone; somehow he knows we're here. This is a slick bastard we're dealing with."

Dt John: "We'll try again tomorrow."

Detective Lucy removes her wig and heads for her car. The other three cars start heading away from the area. As Lucy enters her car, she gets on the radio.

Dt Lucy: "Goodnight, guys."

Dt Joe: "'Night, Lucy, see you tomorrow."

Dt Benny: "'Night, Lu."

Detective Lucy turns the key to start the car and is about to shift into drive. Her movement is interrupted by a wire that has been suddenly wrapped around her neck with extreme pressure. Her only thought right now is to breathe, as she suddenly starts gasping for air. A set of arms are preventing her from releasing the restraint that is now cutting her air supply. With her hands struggling desperately to release the wire from her neck, her strength starts to fade and darkness overtakes her. The next day she is found slumped over the passenger side of her car.

FADE TO OFFICE OF PSYCHIC CINDY

Psychic Cindy: "So, how are you otherwise?"

G-Spot: "Okay. I'm having a lot of good sex."

Psychic Cindy: "Isn't this what you wanted?"

G-Spot: "Yeah, but that's not why I'm here. I'm working on a case and I wanted to get your advice."

Psychic Cindy: "Okay. Come on; tell me what's on your mind."

G-Spot: "I'm thinking of going undercover and I'm a bit nervous about this one."

Psychic Cindy: "Use your ability, have faith in what you do. Keep away from total darkness and you should be fine."

G-Spot: "What do you mean, 'total darkness?'"

Psychic Cindy: "I sense that there is a threat from darkness. Keep to the light. Have faith in your ability. Remember, you have been blessed with powers for a reason."

FADE TO CHIEF TENAFLY'S OFFICE

Chief Tenafly: "I have to tell you, G, that this is a risky job. If you want to back out of this, I'll understand. So far we lost three victims and one female police officer. This perp may be responsible for a lot more than we know. We have dozens of unsolved cases that may be tied to him."

G-Spot: "That's exactly why I have to do this. Detective Lucy and I were at the investigations firm together years ago. She was my friend. I'm going to miss her dearly. This guy has to be caught."

Chief Tenafly: "You'll be wearing a panic button alarm. Don't hesitate to use it if you get in trouble. The boys will be out there in force. You won't see us, but we'll be there. We can't get too close. Don't want to spook this perp. I know you're going to do well. Good luck, G."

G-Spot: "Thanks, Chief."

FADE TO FINAL UNDERCOVER OPERATION

Most of the rapes occurred after sundown. As the crew waits for sundown, G-Spot is driven to the area several blocks away. She feels a bit of anxiety coming over her as she adjusts her makeup.

G-Spot: "Got to tell you, this fake skin is itchy as hell."

Dt Benny: "Can't pass for Hasidic unless you're white."

Dt Joe: "Hey, they don't have Jiffy Pop booty, either, but in this case it may help."

G-Spot: "Don't make me laugh—you're going to ruin my makeup! The prosthetic makeup feels hot as hell, too."

Dt John: "Let's be serious. We're going to be several blocks away."

Dt Joe: "You'll be alone. This guy is like a snake. Comes out of nowhere."

Dt John: "Be careful. Don't take anything for granted."

Dt Benny: "If he approaches you, keep talking into your mic."

Dt John: "If for any reason you can't speak, make sure you can reach your alarm button."

Dt Benny: "We'll be close by, so don't hesitate to press that alarm."

FADE TO FINAL SCENE

With five unmarked cars and several police cars on alert, the team nervously waits for the signal from G-Spot. The area around downtown has a mixture of dark and heavily lit streets. The attacks have been along the Lexington Monmouth area. G-Spot's area of coverage is from Second to Fourteenth streets.

G-Spot heads along her route for the third time carrying an oversize purse. It's 5:30 p.m. as she approaches Fifth Street. Its fall, so sundown comes early. She hears a noise from behind her. She looks but no one is there. Over her mic she whispers,

G-Spot: "Thought I heard something. All I see is a homeless gray-haired dude with a shopping cart full of clothes."

Chief Tenafly: "Be careful. Watch your back."

Continuing her route, G-Spot pretends to ignore the noise as she approaches a playground area. As she passes a large oak tree, she is unaware that her movements are being timed. A homeless man with a shopping cart passes her by. G-Spot realizes that as this homeless person is going by, he lacks the bad odor that usually comes with homeless people.

Before she has time to digest that oddity, a wire is around her neck and she is being dragged toward the tree, away from the streetlight. She drops the purse to grab the end of the wire.

G-Spot struggles to reach for the alarm but she needs her strength to fight, as every second the wire seems to get tighter. G-Spot's mind goes to what the psychic told her: "Keep away from the darkness."

G-Spot notices a car parked next to the streetlight. As she struggles with the perp, she moves in the direction of the vehicle. The perp, unaware of her intentions, moves in the direction of the car for cover. She is about four feet from the car under the streetlight.

The perp and G-Spot are now on the side of the vehicle as G-Spot maneuvers her head toward the side window. She moves her head up and now sees her reflection in the window.

As the perp looks up, his eyes meet hers in the reflection. The wire around G-Spot's neck is suddenly released as G-Spot's trance takes immediate hold of the perp. Because her life was in danger, her trance on the perp is held for an extended and intense period. The perp drops to the ground, as the effect of three hundred orgasms is too much for his heart.

G-Spot, unable to talk, sets off her panic alarm. The area around Fifth and Monmouth is suddenly engulfed with flashing lights and sirens as the team moves in.

CHIEF TENAFLY: "Are you all right, G?" G-spot, still massaging her
   neck, responds,

G-SPOT: "Yeah, I'll be all right, just need a sec."

Detective Tenafly has the standby ambulance help her inside to make sure she is checked out. They hold a respirator to her to give her help in breathing.

DT JOE: "Gee, looks like this guy went out happy. Died with a serious
   hard-on. Jes#s, this was a big motherf##ker! How did you take
   down a guy this big, G?"

DT JOHN: "Looks like he's wearing some kind of mask."

DT BENNY: "Remove it."

Detective Joe grabs at the skin that is coming off and the fake gray hair, removes it to reveal the perp's true identity.

DT JOE: "A handsome-looking kind of guy, hmm."

As detective Joe removes his mask, G-Spot's eyes behind her respirator enlarge. She removes the respirator and yells, "It can't be!!! John?"

EPILOGUE

The investigation leads the team to search John's apartment, where they find a trunk in his closet. They find a collection of panties from every woman he has raped and murdered. The count stopped at about twenty-five pairs. Inside the trunk police find a spool of wire, cutters, and skin-making material. G-Spot is given a special commendation from the mayor and becomes a lifetime friend to the Orthodox community in a small New Jersey town.

FADE TO OFFICE OF PSYCHIC CINDY

PSYCHIC CINDY: "Your heart is bad, G?"

G-SPOT: "I know the things he did were evil, but I still kind of miss him."

PSYCHIC CINDY: "I know, but you did well. Sometimes when one does a good deed, there's a sacrifice that comes with it. You definitely have a good future ahead. After all, you're only thirty-two years old. You have a very special gift. There's a reason why you were given this gift. Your heart will mend."

G-SPOT: "Guess you're right; I got a hot date with JR tonight."

PSYCHIC CINDY: "There you go, girl! That's the spirit. I'll pray for you tonight."

MY CLOSET OR YOURS?

A small Chihuahua name Eddie gets up on his hind legs, pushes a door, and stands before its owner, Mateo. Mateo and Kiel lie in bed locked in a sexual embrace, grinding their pelvic from side to side. Their legs are saturated with the flow of semen. Kiel opens his eyes momentarily and unlocks his lips from Mateo's.

KIEL: "Look who's here, Mateo!"

MATEO: "Uh."

Mateo pauses after a few more kisses to his lover and turns his head around.

MATEO: "Eddie! Can I get some kind of privacy!!? Jesus, can't a brother get some tail? Eddie, I don't know what I'm going to do with you. Next time stay in your own room."

Eddie lets out three barks as if to say kiss my butt, and heads to his room.

FADE TO FULL STORY

A very feminine black man waits for his name to be called as he sits outside the office of Psychic Cindy. This is not his first visit to his advisor. Mateo is a thirty-eight-year-old black man who works in a women's hair salon. People know him by his incredible smile. Even with two missing front teeth, he still manages to smile with pride. Mateo always wears belts with sparkling buckles. A closet queen, Mateo gets a lot of male visitors at his job, but denies his sexual orientation. He deliberately has girls calling him at the salon to throw people off. Mateo's favorite pastime is the nightlife, dancing, and clubs. His whole life revolves around Eddie, his Chihuahua. If Eddie doesn't like you, then Mateo won't trust you.

Eddie, his black tan Chihuahua, is treated like a king and gets away with almost anything. This dog has been in two commercials and two movies. Mateo hears his name called and enters Psychic Cindy's office.

PSYCHIC CINDY: "Good morning Mateo, have a seat. How can I help you today?"

MATEO: "Cindy, it's so good to see you!"

PSYCHIC CINDY: "Nice to see you, Mateo. What's up with you? Where's Eddie?"

MATEO: "I left him home. He's become a TV addict. He just loves Fox news. Cindy, I've been having some bad dreams, and I haven't been able to sleep."

PSYCHIC CINDY: "What about sleeping pills from your doctor?"

MATEO: "They don't work on me. I still have nightmares."

PSYCHIC CINDY: "Tell me about these nightmares."

MATEO: "In my dreams I wake up and I'm not really awake. When I get up, I'm wearing women's clothing. When I try to move I can't, because I'm tied up."

PSYCHIC CINDY: "Why do you think you're having this dream?"

MATEO: "Don't know. I am a straight man, you know."

Cindy's smile widens before she responds:

PSYCHIC CINDY: "Yes, I know, Mateo. I think your dream represents your alter ego."

MATEO: "What does that mean?"

PSYCHIC CINDY: "Nothing bad. There's a part of you that is struggling to get out. Don't worry; you don't have to wear women's clothing. Just be yourself, Mateo. You're going to be tested this month, and it is going to be a life-changing event. You're okay, Mateo. Everything will be fine. That dream will be gone in a few weeks. No need to stress over it."

FADE TO THE GENTLEMAN'S CLUB

Mateo and a guy name Christian are on the dance floor. They're discussing a guy Mateo met at the club.

CHRISTIAN: "So, what else did he say to you, Mateo?"

MATEO: "He told me about the law firm he works for and a big case that he is working on."

CHRISTIAN: "What kind of case is this?"

MATEO: "Don't know yet. But it's an important one."

CHRISTIAN: "Gee, you got yourself a lawyer, Mateo."

MATEO: "But he was checking out my butt every time I moved around. I caught him looking."

CHRISTIAN: "A bottom feeder. Hmm, sounds sweet. Is he cute?"

MATEO: "Yeah, he's adorable. He's got green eyes and blond hair. He's 'bout six feet tall. Nice arms and big chest. I'll be seeing him tonight. There's one other thing about him that I share."

CHRISTIAN: "What's that?"

MATEO: "He's as much in the closet as I am. Maybe more so."

CHRISTIAN: "Oh, what does that mean?"

MATEO: "No one at his firm knows that he's gay. He would lose his job and position if they found out."

Mateo meets Kiel at his place near a redone warehouse in SoHo. Mateo is dressed in his open black silk shirt, skin-tight pants, and blue velvet shoes. Mateo presses the doorbell and stares at the lenses of a camera above the door. Two seconds later a buzzer goes off. Mateo takes the elevator. When it reaches the seventh floor, Kiel opens the door; Mateo is spraying himself with a pinkie-size bottle of perfume.

KIEL: "Is that for me? Honey, you already smell sweet enough. Glad you could make it."

MATEO: "Why wouldn't I? Did you miss me?"

KIEL: "Of course, baby. I want you."

MATEO: "Can you show me?"

KIEL: "Slow down, baby. The night is young."

Mateo gives Kiel a hug and lands a soft kiss on his lips. As Kiel and Mateo move to the living room area, Mateo notices that one wall is heavily decorated with Kiel's awards and educational degrees. Kiel pours a drink for Mateo.

MATEO: "You're pretty hot shit with all these degrees and things."

KIEL: "What do you mean?"

MATEO: "I mean, it makes me wonder."

KIEL: "It makes you wonder about what?"

MATEO: "Why you want to be with someone like me."

KIEL: "Because…Oh stop, degrees are just pieces of paper, Mateo.
I know guys who have Master's and Ph.D.'s and they are
lost bitches. It has nothing to do with who you really are."

Mateo can't help but feel butterflies in his stomach as he begins to
look at this man in a different way. Mateo notices a document on the table
with notes on it.

MATEO: "Is that what you're working on now?"

KIEL: "Yeah, some lady shot her husband eight times."

MATEO: "Gee."

KIEL: "Claims it was self-defense."

MATEO: "Self-defense?"

KIEL: "Yep, she reloaded the gun and shot him three more times."

MATEO: "You're defending her?"

KIEL: "A Victoria Davis. I've been given the pleasure of doing the
impossible. What I'm about to tell you is confidential, so keep it
to yourself, please."

Kiel describes Victoria's account of the homicide.

FADE BACK TO THE DAY OF THE CRIME

A small woman of 110 pounds, about 5-feet-2, is struggling to keep a
bedroom door closed. A 250-pound man on the other side is gaining
leverage in pushing the door open.

VICTORIA: "Danny! No, leave me alone!"

DANNY: "I told you before never to lock the f##cking door, bitch! You
want to f@#k with me? I'll show you who to f#@k with!"

Danny swings his fist back and punches a hole through the door.
Victoria catches part of the impact as his fist comes in contact with the
side of her head. With one final push the husband shoves open the door,
knocking his wife against a bureau.

VICTORIA: "You bastard!"

Danny grabs Victoria by the hair and picks her up with his right arm.
Victoria is now face to face with him and kicks him in the groin. As he
reacts to the kick and falls back, he throws her back against the bureau.

Victoria, bruised and hurt from the impact to her back, is losing her strength and feeling weak. With her back to her husband, she reaches inside a drawer and retrieves a handgun. The husband, with one hand to his groin, starts to come back at her to continue his attack. Victoria turns around now facing her husband.

VICTORIA: "You piece of shit!"

She fires and keeps firing until the gun is empty. As the bullets make impact with his body, Danny falls back and is in shock, but has a grin on his face. Victoria reaches back into the drawer and grabs the remaining three bullets. She nervously reloads the gun.

Danny, already shot five times, continues to come at Victoria with a final attempt to silence her. Victoria points the gun at him once again and fires the three remaining bullets. One bullet enters his head.

FADE BACK TO KIEL AND MATEO

MATEO: "It seems clear that it was self-defense."

KIEL: "Not that simple. She reloaded the gun! Anyway, if I win this case
    for the firm, it means better things for me."

MATEO: "I'm sure you'll do fine. Are you hungry?"

KIEL: "A little bit."

MATEO: "How about I make you something to eat? I'm a pretty good
    cook."

KIEL: "Okay, let me show you where things are in the kitchen."

MATEO: "No, no, no! I know my way around a kitchen. Just relax, I'll be
    fine."

Mateo is busy in the kitchen making a beef stew dinner. A restless Kiel sits in the den pondering about his future, while looking over his notes. His mind starts to wander away from work and his other senses take over. Kiel gets up and moves toward Mateo, who has his back to him.

KIEL: "How are you doing, Mateo?"

MATEO: "Just fine. You have all the ingredients I need."

Kiel leans over, grabs Mateo by the waist, and gives him a love hug. He places a wet kiss behind his right ear. As Mateo reacts to Kiel's touch, Kiel becomes aroused. Mateo feels a growing erection against his rear.

MATEO: "Maybe I should adjust the flame on this for slow cooking. Seems like your appetite has changed a bit."

As Kiel reaches down and starts to rub Mateo's groin area, Mateo begins to perspire. Mateo turns around and plants his lips across Mateo mouth. With Mateo's erect penis in his hand, Kiel walks him toward his bedroom. Mateo reaches over and grabs Kiel's penis.

MATEO: "I want this mother##ker in me now."

KIEL: "Baby, those words are music to my ears."

Kiel positions Mateo with his hands down and his butt up in the air and enters him as Mateo lets out the beginning of many moans. Pain turns to pleasure for Mateo. Twenty minutes later, Kiel is near the point of orgasm. Reacting to Mateo's moans, he explodes his load into Mateo and lays there on top of him.

FADE TO OFFICE OF BENSON AND BENSON

KIEL: "Good morning, Mr. Benson. I understand you wanted to see me?"

MR. BENSON: "Yes, Kiel, come in. Have a seat. Kiel, I'm very happy with the way you have been handling the Davis case. The fact is there's a five-hundred-thousand-dollar defense fee in this case. We do well with this one, means many more behind it. I'm not going to bullshit you about this. We're thinking of bringing you on as a full partner. There are benefits with that, of course."

KIEL: "I'll do my best not to disappoint you."

MR. BENSON: "There's one more thing!"

KIEL: "What's that, Mr. Benson?"

MR. BENSON: "My partners are a bit old-fashioned. They believe in the sanctity of marriage! It would be a lot easier to promote a married man, if you get my meaning. Have you ever thought of marrying that gal you've been seeing?"

KIEL: "Susan?"

MR. BENSON: "Yes, that's the one. Susan."

KIEL: "I'm working on it."

MR. BENSON: "Well, sounds like you need to work a little harder. Maybe the three of us could meet for dinner sometime?"

KIEL: "I'll talk to her next time I see her."

As the Davis case goes to trial, Kiel prepares and gathers all evidence and witnesses. He calls to the stand all witnesses who have known the Davis family and their turbulent history. One by one, as the witnesses testify for Victoria, the case starts to take shape. The fact that she reloaded the weapon is a big factor in the plaintiff family's claim. Kiel investigates and finds that Mr. Davis had a history of domestic violence in his previous marriages. Kiel decides to subpoena Mr. Davis's other wives and past girlfriends.

Kiel meets Mateo at his apartment and stays overnight. During their love conversation, Kiel tells Mateo that the firm has extended an offer for a partnership. Mateo is puzzled and doesn't understand the meaning of it, but for the first time feels uneasy about his relationship with Kiel. Kiel is not being honest, but the position with the firm would look better if the person was married. Unknown to Mateo, Kiel is making plans to marry someone in his firm he's been dating on the side. Kiel doesn't love Susan, but knows that it would be a good career move.

Mateo's dog, Eddie, starts barking at Kiel for the first time. Eddie grabs Kiel's pants and starts to shake them side to side. He runs into his room with Kiel's pants in his mouth.

MATEO: "That's strange. I thought he'd be used to you by now."

KIEL: "Eddie, what's wrong?"

KIEL: "Mateo, I have something that I have to tell you."

MATEO: "What is it?"

KIEL: "The firm that I work for is thinking of making me a partner."

MATEO: "What does that mean?"

KIEL: "Besides more money, I also participate in decisions that affect the firm."

MATEO: "That's what you wanted, yes? What are you saying?"

KIEL: "Just saying that, I don't know what this is going to mean for us. I'm just saying that maybe I need a break."

MATEO: "You need a break. What about us?"

KIEL: "Yeah, I mean I have a lot to juggle right now. Maybe we could both use a break. I don't like deception any more than you do. Don't worry—one day we'll be together and out of the closet."

MATEO: "Swear?"

KIEL: "I promise."

Mateo begins to grow suspicious of Kiel .While Eddie was shaking Kiel's pants, Kiel's wallet fell out and landed on the floor. Eddie picked up a business card that slipped out of the wallet and brought it to Mateo. On one side is a name and phone number and on the other is the name "Susan." Mateo finds out about Kiel's secret dates with Susan and decides to confront him. Kiel tries to explain to Mateo that it's not over, that it's just a marriage of convenience for the opportunity of a lifetime to become a full partner with the firm.

MATEO: "But you promised me, Kiel!"

KIEL: "Mateo, it's just until I get the offer. Do you know how long I've waited for this?"

MATEO: "What about Susan?"

KIEL: "What about Susan? She means nothing to me. I'm going to have her sign a prenuptial."

MATEO: "How does she feel about this?"

KIEL: "It doesn't matter how she feels. Do you think I'll let some bitch get between us?"

Mateo is unable to sleep that night. As he tosses and turns in his bed, all he can think about is Kiel. Mateo wants to visit Kiel's office and expose his gay lifestyle. He knows this will not only piss off Kiel but also get him fired. Deep down inside he knows it's an immature thing to do, but he can't help playing the scenario over and over in his head. He sees himself busting open the door and the look on Kiel's face.

FADE TO THE OFFICE OF BENSON AND BENSON

Mateo is outside in the hallway with his hand on the doorknob. The glass on the door has the words BENSON AND BENSON engraved into it.

HEART TO HEART

OPENING SCENE

The scene opens up to a helicopter view of Cinque Terre beach in Italy. As the view zooms in, you begin to see a couple under a secluded area of the beach making love as the sun is going down.

Song "Forever Begins Tonight" by Patrizio Buanne

FADE TO FULL STORY
ELISA IN HER ROOM IN STATEN ISLAND

A tenacious sixth-grader, Elisa is oblivious to everything around her as she finishes a doll sketch on her homework pad.

MOM: "Elisa, hurry up or you'll miss the bus! Your brother is already outside."

ELISA: "But, Mama, can't I finish my drawing?"

MOM: "If you miss your bus, I'm not taking you to school. I don't know why you waste time scribbling. Your brother always has his homework done on time."

Elisa tears off the drawings from her pad, leaves them on her desk. She puts her pad away in her book bag and runs downstairs.

MOM: "If you don't keep up, you will grow up and be nothing."

ELISA: "Don't you like my drawings?"

MOM: "I don't want you wasting time with nonsense."

ELISA: "Aren't you proud of me, Mama?"

MOM: "Hurry up, your bus is here. Go. Don't forget your books."

After Elisa gets on the bus, her mom goes to her daughter's room. She picks up the drawings, pauses for a few second to look at them. "Cartoons!" she says. "My daughter is drawing cartoons! Hmm, I swear this one will grow up to be nothing."

She grabs the sketches and dumps them outside in the garbage.

A tall man of average build with a thin mustache and goatee claps his hands three times to get the attention of his class.

PROFESSOR: "Okay, people, can I have your attention? This is a good example of how to drape the fabric over your dress forms. I want everyone to look at Elisa's dress form. You must understand how fabric falls on the human body. If you cannot understand this, you will not be a good designer. Remember, class: the habits you form here you take with you into the industry. Practice, practice, practice, these till you get it right. I don't want you to say you learned bad habits from professor Haney at F.I.T. Good job, Elisa."

ELISA: "Thank you."

OUTSIDE OF CLASS AT A STUDENT GATHERING ON THE ROOF OF BUILDING D

SUSAN: "Elisa, I was trying to get your attention but you left so fast after class."

ELISA: "Yeah, I had to go meet my brother Tony."

SUSAN: "I was wondering if we could get together and share ideas. I'm having some trouble with my dress form; maybe I could see how you drape it."

ELISA: "Okay, but when?"

SUSAN: "I have a dress form at home."

ELISA: "Okay, let me know when's a good time for you, but it has to be before the spring break."

SUSAN: "Where are you going for spring break, Elisa?"

ELISA: "I'm going to where I always go, Italy!"

SUSAN: "Italy! Wow. Sounds nice. Is your family from there?"

ELISA: "Yep. In Monterosso al Mare. Can't wait to see them."

FADE TO INTERNATIONAL AIRPORT IN ROME

Elisa is greeted at the gate by her cousin Adrianna. When the two meet, they embrace and share tears of joy.

ADRIANNA: "How are things with you, Elisa?"

ELISA: "Not bad. I am so happy to see you, cousin."

ADRIANNA: "So tell me, have you met anyone at that college you go to?"

ELISA: "It's my first year there. I have a few friends. That's why I need to get away."

ADRIANNA: "Why, are you afraid of guys?"

ELISA: "No, silly, I needed a break because it's my first year at college."

ADRIANNA: "What about your family? What about Mama and Papa?"

ELISA: "Oh, they never change. They're okay. Papa's still working hard."

ADRIANNA: "And Mama?"

ELISA: "Still the same. I don't want to talk about her."

ADRIANNA: "I know, but you can always count on me, Elisa."

ELISA: "I know I can."

ADRIANNA: "You're right; it's time to think Italy!"

Adrianna gives her cousin a big hug, holds on to her tight, and kisses her on the side of her head.

ADRIANNA: "I'm so happy to see you, Elisa!"

ELISA: "I love coming here. I'm happy to see you, too."

ADRIANNA: "There's a big beach party going on tonight on Cinque Terre strip. You definitely are going."

ELISA: "What about us spending some time with your parents? I'd like to spend some time with Don Pepe and Donna Fina."

ADRIANNA: "What are you talking about?"

ELISA: "They expect me to spend time with them. I don't want to be rude."

ADRIANNA: "Don't worry about that. They also want you to enjoy yourself while you're here. They'll understand."

ELISA: "It not like in America."

ADRIANNA: "They know how young people behave. They were once young like us."

ELISA: "Yeah, I guess you're right."

ADRIANNA: "Besides, you're going to be with us for two weeks. Don't worry; we'll see them before we go out."

ELISA: "How's your brother Emilio?"

ADRIANNA: "Still the same. Emilio, he never changes."

The drive to Monterroso al Mare is long. Elisa, exhausted from jet lag, falls asleep and awakes to find Adrianna's brother Berto and the parents greet her as she exits the car.

ELISA: "Hi, Emilio, look at you. Oh my God, you're so big! You even have a mustache!"

EMILIO: "That's man stuff. Hey, Elisa, you turned into a babe! America has been good for you, no?"

ELISA: "Come here, gotta hug you for that one, cuz!"

Emilio, not very affectionate, is taken back by Elisa's hug but returns a hug as well.

ELISA: "Your English has improved."

EMILIO: "I take classes at the university."

ELISA: "Buena será, Don Pepe. Esta toda vis joven."

DON PEPE: "Grazie, va bene cosí. Su madre, su padre, Elisa??

ELISA: "Sonó en bueno statu de salud. Grazie."

Elisa smiles and hugs Don Pepe and turns to hug his wife, Donna Fina, who is waiting to greet her.

ELISA: "How are you, Donna Fina? I'm so happy to see you!"

DONNA FINA: "Why, Elisa, you blossomed into a beautiful woman!"

ELISA: "Thank you, that's so kind of you."

DONNA FINA: "Fa Como faccia a casa tua."

FADE TO THE BEACH PARTY SCENE AT CINQUE TERRE

Elisa, Adrianna, and Emilio are on the beach sitting at a table sipping sciacchetra in an area where young people their age gather. You can smell the anchovies fresh from the sea. Nearby in the town, traditional music is playing as seafood freshly taken from the sea is cooked.

ADRIANNA: "Hey, Elisa, you never told me if you have a boyfriend."

Elisa pauses from taking a sip on a glass of sciacchetra to answer.

ELISA: "Nobody special right now. A few dates."

EMILIO: "I have a friend you might like."

ELISA: "Emilio, you haven't changed a bit! Always trying to hook me up with one of your buddies."

EMILIO: "Elisa, are they all that bad? What about Donate?"

ELISA: "I remember when you introduced me to your friend Donate. How can I forget Donate? I was waiting for Donate to look up in the air and say, 'The plane, boss. The plane is here!'"

EMILIO: "He was a nice guy, no?"

ELISA: "Yeah, if you like guys who are four feet tall!"

EMILIO: "I know this guy, Berto. I think you'll like him."

ADRIANNA: "Oh my God, Elisa, you got to meet Berto! I swear to God, if it wasn't for my boyfriend I'd take him myself."

EMILIO: "He'll be here soon. You'll get to meet him."

ELISA: "Gee, I can't wait. Does he have hair?"

As the three of them sit there and chat, they start on their second bottle of dessert wine. In the distance walking along the beach, a tall Steve Reeves–looking guy is heading their way, waving at Emilio and Adrianna. Emilio is the first one to notice Berto.

EMILIO: "There he is now!"

ELISA: "Who is 'he'?"

EMILIO: "It's Berto, the guy I was talking about."

Elisa's eye catches his from a distance, and she seems to fall into a trance. As Berto comes closer to the group, he too cannot seem to take his eyes off Elisa.

Song: "A Natural High" by Bloodstone

When Berto reaches the table, he reaches over to shake Emilio's hand but his eyes are still on Elisa.

BERTO: "You didn't tell me you had a guest."

EMILIO: "Berto, this is Elisa, my cousin from New York. Elisa, this is my friend Berto."

Elisa reaches over to shake Berto's hand. Adrianna, not one to miss anything, finally opens her mouth.

ADRIANNA: "Hello, Berto, remember me? Hello?"

BERTO: "Hi, Adrianna. How are you doing?"

Berto, still holding on to Elisa's hand, can't help but joke at her affection.

BERTO: "Can you give me back my hand?"

ELISA: "Oh, sorry, of course."

BERTO: "Just kidding. Your hand is very nice."

Adrianna and Emilio are all smiles as they now find themselves alone while Berto and Elisa are momentarily stuck for words but seem to share a trance of attraction. Adrianna decides to have a nicotine attack.

ADRIANNA: "Emilio, can you walk me to get some cigarettes at the bar?"

EMILIO: "When did you start smoking?"

Under the table, Adrianna gives Emilio a big kick to the ankle.

EMILIO: "Ouch, shit! Okay, now I remember you started yesterday. Okay, I go with you."

While Adrianna and Emilio take an extended trip to buy cigarettes, Berto and Elisa are finally alone.

BERTO: "Elisa, do you understand my English?"

ELISA: "Your English is as good as my Italian, so that makes us even. No se pre occupi."

BERTO: "How long are you here for?"

ELISA: "Just two weeks. I usually come with my parents, but this time they couldn't make it. Do you live far from here?"

BERTO: "I live in Capri, but the beach is better here, no?"

ELISA: "I think so."

BERTO: "Would you like to go for a walk? We come back before end of sun, okay? I promise I won't bite you!"

ELISA: "Okay."

Berto extends his hand and Elisa grabs and holds on to him as if she has known him for years. They walk along the beach and continue to stimulate their attraction as the afternoon takes its time to change to evening. For a while they say very little to each other as they take in the beauty of the Liguria cliffs. Most of their attraction for each other is being said in the variation in how they hold each other's hands. For some reason, the scenery looks different today than in previous years. It's the type of look that things take on when the heart is involved more than the mind.

By the time they get back to the beachfront, Adrianna and Emilio are waiting by their table. Berto had Elisa laughing at the stories he told her, and she seemed to be more relaxed than in the beginning. Elisa is careful not to open up her heart to soon. She avoids giving him the impression that she is his.

That night she wonders if he has had other women. After all, he is an incredibly handsome man and turned many heads when they walked along the beach. It had been a long time since Elisa had had thoughts these kinds of thoughts toward a man. Maybe it was all a dream. Maybe she would get up in the morning and be in New York. That was her final thought as sleep took over her.

FADE TO BERTO'S APARTMENT

Berto called Emilio as soon as he got home to thank him for the nice time he had at the beach outing. Emilio, being the joker, said that he and Adrianna bought a lot of cigarettes. Berto told his friend that he had never seen a more beautiful woman in his life. He asked him if they were going to bring her back the next day. He was careful and shy about his attraction to Elisa, yet there were feelings that were taking over his shyness. In the back of his mind, he also knew that she was only going to be here for less than two weeks now.

Would he allow his heart to be open only to be closed again after two weeks? Did she have someone waiting for her back in the States? These questions kept coming up in his mind, and he knew that eventually he would find out one way or another. After all, life was very simple for him compared to life in the States. He was accustomed to the Old Italian ways of courtship and had pride and confidence that these ways would still work for him. But he was getting way ahead of himself. What was he thinking? After all, he just met her!

TWO WEEKS LATER

This would be the last day before the end of vacation for Elisa. It would be another year before she would be with her family, so she wanted to spend the day with them. She had spent most of the vacation enjoying her family and newfound friend, Berto .Now there was a sadness that crept over these remaining days of her vacation, as she realized that once again she would be in the hustle and bustle of city life. But most of all, she had developed a deep attraction for Berto and knew that this was something special. This was something that could develop into more than just a friendship. For now she had to concentrate on her career and what lies ahead.

Emilio and Adrianna drive her to the airport with Don Pepe and Donna Fina. There is no sign of Berto. Berto does not feel comfortable with goodbyes. Adrianna tries to comfort Elisa by telling her that he probably missed the one bus that ran to the airport and was unable to get a ride.

As Elisa checks her baggage, time is moving faster than ever before. In fifteen minutes she will be boarding the plane; it is time to say her goodbyes. Elisa hugs Don Pepe and Donna Fina, thanking them for their hospitality and home. Adrianna gives Elisa a longer than usual hug.

ADRIANNA: "Elisa, call me when you get home—don't forget! Love you, cuz."

ELISA: "Love you, too. Stay away from those cigarettes!"

Holding back her tears, Adrianna pauses a moment and then laughs as she recalls the scene at the beach with the cigarettes. Emilio, not being affectionate, for the first time urges his sister to give him some time with Elisa.

EMILIO: "Come on, Adrianna, don't hog the goodbye—she's running out of time!"

Emilio gives his cousin an awkward but very affectionate hug. He lands a kiss on her cheek.

ELISA: "Goodbye, Emilio, thanks for making my stay a great one. If you see Berto, let him know I said goodbye."

EMILIO: "I will. Hey, cousin! You are coming back next year, right?"

ELISA: "Absolutely."

As the final call for boarding is called, Elisa grabs her carry-on and gets on line behind the gate to board her plane.

Meanwhile Berto was able to hop a ride to the airport and just arrived. With only minutes left, he thanks his driver for the lift and makes a mad run to the departure area for the New York flights.

He runs into Emilio, Adrianna, and the parents coming out.

EMILIO: "Berto! She's already on line for boarding. What happened to you?"

EMILIO: "I waited as long as I could."

EMILIO: "If you hurry, you might see her before she boards!"

Berto spots her as he nears the boarding area. He yells out her name: "Elisa!!! Elisa!!!"

Elisa thinks she is hearing things and turns around to look. A smile replaces her frown.

ELISA: "Berto!!"

Elisa gets off the line and stands there, dropping her carry-on to the floor. Berto reaches her and pauses to catch his breath.

BERTO: "I needed to say goodbye to you."

Berto reaches and grabs her hands gently as the two are face to face in their love trance.

BERTO: "I've been thinking about you all the time. Can't get you out of my mind."

ELISA: "I've been thinking about you, too."

BERTO: "You are back maybe next year?"

ELISA: "You going to be here?"

BERTO: "Of course."

ELISA: "Then I'll be back. You better call me."

Elisa puts her arms around Berto's waist and says,

ELISA: "We're running out of time—you better kiss me, fool!"

Berto moves closer to Elisa and their lips meet for a heartfelt farewell kiss. What seems like a minute feels like eternity to them. The last person on line for boarding has left and the flight attendant reminds Elisa that the time for boarding has ended.

FLIGHT ATTENDANT: "Madame, we need to board now!"

Elisa picks up her hand luggage and turns around to enter the ramp to the plane.

BERTO: "Elisa, what about your number?"

Elisa yells from the ramp...

ELISA: "Adrianna or Emilio has the number!"

A now more confident Elisa floats down the hallway leading to the door of the plane. As if a great weight has been taken off her shoulder, a glow seems to be all around her.....

ONE WEEK LATER
THE OFFICE OF PSYCHIC CINDY

PSYCHIC CINDY: "Well, Elisa, I'm happy to see you. It's been a while. How was your vacation? How was Italy? I feel excitement coming from you!"

ELISA: "Cindy, I have so much to tell you. I had a great time. I didn't want it to end."

PSYCHIC CINDY: "I feel there is something maybe more that happened. You seem to be much happier."

ELISA: "Well, I have to tell you, I met this guy."

PSYCHIC CINDY: "Okay."

ELISA: "Cindy, something happened to me."

PSYCHIC CINDY: "You've got my attention."

ELISA: "I just can't stop thinking of him. I need to know if he's the one."

PSYCHIC CINDY: "Well, I think that you answered that already. Tell me more about him."

ELISA: "Well, he's extremely handsome, kind, and gentle."

PSYCHIC CINDY: "Handsome is always a plus."

ELISA: "Just learning to speak English. Kind of old school, traditional. He's a painter."

PSYCHIC CINDY: "Fine art?"

ELISA: "No, specialized painting. Most of all he makes me feel good whenever I'm around him. Makes me feel confident, like there's nothing I can't do."

PSYCHIC CINDY: "Elisa, you're giving me goose bumps—stop it! I'm very happy for you. Does he have a brother? Just kidding! Have you told your mother about him?"

ELISA: "I am always careful about what I tell my mom. Somehow she sensed or picked up Berto's vibes."

PSYCHIC CINDY: "How?"

ELISA: "Don't know, but I'm not ready to tell her."

PSYCHIC CINDY: "Women know when other women are in love."

ELISA: "I don't want her to bring me down from my cloud."

PSYCHIC CINDY: "I see. What about Dad?"

ELISA: "Dad? Not ready to tell dad."

PSYCHIC CINDY: "And your career—how's that going?"

ELISA: "School is going good for me, and I'm getting better at what I do. I got a part-time job working at a designer studio."

PSYCHIC CINDY: "Sounds like you have everything under control. Most of all, sounds like you have control of your destiny. Not everyone can make that claim. My door is always open to you. Let me know how you're doing. Keep in touch. I'm going to pray for you. Don't forget: I like to hear from you, okay?"

FIVE MONTHS LATER, AT THE FASHION INSTITUTE OF TECHNOLO-GY, OUTSIDE OF CLASS, NOONTIME

SUSAN: "You know, that guy Jason, he was asking about you."

ELISA: "Oh?"

SUSAN: "Are you seeing him?"

ELISA: "Just hanging out, nothing serious."

SUSAN: "What about that guy Berto you told me about?"

ELISA: "I was talking to him last night. I think about him all the time."

SUSAN: "But he's far away. How do you deal with that?"

ELISA: "I have a large phone bill!"

SUSAN: "I don't know how you manage without him. If it were me, I'd go out of my mind."

Elisa thought about what Susan said. That night she called Berto. He asked about New York life and schools in New York. His dream was to one day work in the IT field in New York City. He studied information technology in Rome, but he was hyped about the big money and success you can have in the United States.

ELISA: "Berto, I would love to have you here. I have to tell you, the apartments here are quite expensive."

BERTO: "Also, I get to see you, too."

ELISA: "That's sweet. I miss you, too. When are you thinking of moving?"

BERTO: "*Molto presto*—very soon."

Elisa tosses and turns in her bed throughout the night, contemplating all different scenarios. She fears what may happen if her relationship with Berto falters. What would this do to her? How would that affect her career?

On the other hand she knows in her heart that no other man has made her feel what she feels for Berto. Would she lose these feelings seeing him every day?

Unknown to Elisa, Berto has other plans for his sweetheart. His plans involve a future together. He doesn't want to wait for a year to see the girl of his dreams.

Berto decides to follow his dream and his heart. He decides to surprise Elisa and books a flight to New York. While staying at a local hotel, he makes a few important phone calls. It will take a few days, but Berto wants everything to be perfect before he surprises Elisa. Berto knows Elisa's schedule but decides that before he goes to see her, he will call first. He wants to make sure she is at work.

The day arrives and Berto calls Elisa to tell her that he is thinking about her. She thinks it a bit strange at first because of the time but ignores it for the moment.

Berto arrives at Elisa's studio by taxi and waits outside before going in. He pauses, looks up, and looks at his watch for a moment before going in.

Elisa is working on intimate apparel at her studio, checking the fit on one of her designs with a model. The model is clad in a string thong with a demi-cup bra.

Berto arrives at her studio as she is going over instructions on the presentation of the design.

BERTO: "Uh, duh, I never seen that before. I could learn English better maybe with instructor wearing that?"

ELISA: "Berto! Oh my God! How did you get here? Could you please wait outside? Brook, ten minutes—I'll be right back."

MODEL BROOK: "Okay, Elisa."

Elisa comes out to the waiting room and embraces Berto; He returns the embrace with a long kiss. He maintains a funny smile on his face. They hold on and bury themselves in each other's arms. Her emotions are up and down. She is happy but also scared.

ELISA: "Why didn't you let me know you were coming? When did you get here?"

BERTO: "About four days ago. I'm at Cortland Hotel on Seventh Avenue. I came to America to see you. I could not wait another year. I have a surprise for you."

ELISA: "You came all this way to give me a gift? You could have mailed it, silly! I'm so happy you're here."

Berto looks at his watch and grabs Elisa's hand.

BERTO: "Come with me."

ELISA: "What?"

He walks her outside and looks up at the sky.

BERTO: "Look, Elisa, look over there!"

Elisa looks up and sees a media blimp with a message on it. As it gets closer she can see it reads, WILL YOU MARRY ME?

PSYCHIC CINDY

OPENING SCENE

A woman is screaming hysterically into the phone, barely making any sense as I awake from a much-needed two-hour nap. I shake the sleep off and grab my phone from the charger.

PSYCHIC CINDY: "Hello?"

UNKNOWN PERSON: "Hi. Is this Psychic Cindy?"

Psychic Cindy rubs her eyes and yawns before answering.

PSYCHIC CINDY: "Yes. Can I help you? Who is this?"

RAMONA: "Ramona. Demon inside."

PSYCHIC CINDY: "What?"

RAMONA: "Demon inside me."

PSYCHIC CINDY: "Demon?"

RAMONA: "Voices inside my head. I was told you could help me. You're highly recommended from a friend. She said you are the best."

PSYCHIC CINDY: "I don't know if I can help you. It's not what I do. I can make an appointment for you."

RAMONA: "Can I come see you now?"

FADE TO FULL STORY
CLIENT RAMONA CASTRO SESSION ONE

First time I heard from Ramona Castro was over the telephone. She had a harsh deep voice. I sensed a woman in a lot of pain. In person she looks a lot different than what I expected. A portly woman of about 5-foot-3 with matted dark brown hair, she came to me looking like a homeless person. She had on a pair of lace-up shoes, blue polyester one-size-fits-all pants, and a button-up blouse. She had brown eyes with dark circles around them. A thirty-seven year-old woman who looked more like she was fifty-seven. It was apparent that she didn't get much sleep.

PSYCHIC CINDY: "How can I help you, Ramona?"

RAMONA: "I have strangers living inside me. I hear a demon in my head talking."

PSYCHIC CINDY: "What is it saying?"

RAMONA: "To hurt someone."

PSYCHIC CINDY: "Who?"

RAMONA: "Don't know. It's a voice talking to me."

I didn't know if I was getting in over my head with Ramona. I decided to find out if she had any family. This may provide some clue or history to her hysteria. It seemed like the best place to start.

PSYCHIC CINDY: "Tell me about your family."

RAMONA: "My family?"

PSYCHIC CINDY: "Do you come from a big family? Have any brothers, sisters?"

RAMONA: "Two brothers and two sisters. I have not seen them in years."

PSYCHIC CINDY: "And your parents—mother?"

RAMONA: "Mama worked in a plant for many years. She assembled cars for Ford. She worked there before she got sick."

PSYCHIC CINDY: "How so?"

RAMONA: "She developed tuberculosis. She was too sick to take care of us, so we were put in an orphanage in upstate New York. My dad could not take care of us and work at the same time."

PSYCHIC CINDY: "That was very hard on you, I'm sure. What was it like in there?"

FADE TO ST JOSEPH'S HOME, UPSTATE, 29 YEARS AGO

Ramona Castro is on her way to her room. She hears noises coming from the nun's quarters and is distracted. Her curiosity gets the better of her, and she detours to get closer to the sounds of a woman.

As she approaches Sister Helen's room, the sounds get louder. The door to Sister Helen's room is wide open. When Ramona looks, she is shocked by what she sees. Father Powell is on top of Sister Helen. They are both naked and making funny noises. It is the first time she has seen this. She is in a deep stare. Sister Helen turns and catches her looking.

SISTER HELEN: "Oh, shit, one of the kids!"

FATHER POWELL: "Who?"

SISTER HELEN: "Ramona."

By the time Father Powell turns around to look, Ramona is gone. She ran back to the hallway that led to the children's dormitory.

BACK TO PSYCHIC CINDY AND RAMONA

PSYCHIC CINDY: "What happened then?"

RAMONA: "They locked me up in a room for four hours and made me repeat the words 'I did not see anything bad.' I had to repeat it at least a thousand times. They told me if I said anything, they would abuse my younger brother."

PSYCHIC CINDY: "You told no one about this?"

RAMONA: "No one until now."

PSYCHIC CINDY: "How long were you guys there for?"

RAMONA: "Six years."

PSYCHIC CINDY: "What happened?"

RAMONA: "A miracle happened. My mom beat the odds and cheated death. She got better and was able to go home."

PSYCHIC CINDY: "That must have been a happy time."

RAMONA: "It was. At least for a while."

PSYCHIC CINDY: "How did you get along with your dad?"

I could see that I must have struck a nerve because of the look on her face. She closed her eyes and began to shake.

PSYCHIC CINDY: "Are you okay? Ramona? Ramona?" Ramona looks up at me and smiles.

UNKNOWN VOICE: "Who the hell are you???"

PSYCHIC CINDY: "Where's Ramona?"

DEMON JULIA: "Julia, my name's Julia. Don't get me confused with that hobo. It's disgusting to be in this body."

PSYCHIC CINDY: "What happened to Ramona?"

DEMON JULIA: "She's hiding. She's chicken shit, man."

145

Now I had a bigger problem. My client had somehow disappeared. It was her body, but the person talking to me was not her. I wasn't an expert in identity disorders, but I knew I had to at least get Ramona back to where she was. I figure the trigger that brought Julia here was when I brought up memories of her father.

What was the connection between Julia and Ramona? I went with what I had. Julia was obviously the demon that Ramona spoke of, the stranger inside her. The question was, Could I get Ramona back?

PSYCHIC CINDY: "Julia, tell me why you're here."

DEMON JULIA: "Shit, man, I'm here because Ramona is afraid."

PSYCHIC CINDY: "Afraid of what?"

DEMON JULIA: "Afraid of truth."

PSYCHIC CINDY: "Did you have something to do with that?"

DEMON JULIA: "Hell no, her father did that."

PSYCHIC CINDY: "What did he do?"

DEMON JULIA: "You ask a lot of questions, don't you? Who are you?"

PSYCHIC CINDY: "I'm Psychic Cindy. Do you want to help Ramona?"

DEMON JULIA: "Do I look like a helper to you? Why should I?"

PSYCHIC CINDY: "You don't like me saying the word *Ramona*."

The more I say Ramona's name, it seems to affect Julia. I repeat her name several times: "Ramona, Ramona, Ramona."

Ramona seems to snap out of her sleep and now is completely exhausted. Whatever hold this spirit had on her was weakened by the sound of her name. Perhaps it brought to life the fact that Ramona was a real person. Somewhere inside of Ramona, a part of her was fighting back to gain control of her identity.

Because of Ramona's finances, I waived the fees for service. Ramona was desperate to get well and I didn't want to add additional stress because of money. The demon inside Ramona was encouraging her to hurt herself. I had to work quickly to find a way to prevent this from happening.

SESSION TWO

The second time I met with Ramona, my questions were more therapeutic. **PSYCHIC CINDY:** "How are you doing, Ramona?"

RAMONA: "I'm fine. I guess."

PSYCHIC CINDY: "You're very brave to be here. I know it's hard. You will get better. I have to ask you questions that are painful but it will make you better. It's the only way we can get rid of the demons. Tell me what happened after you left the home."

RAMONA: "Do I have to?"

PSYCHIC CINDY: "Yes, you do."

RAMONA: "My mom and dad found a place in upper Manhattan. It was a railway flat with six rooms. The boys had their own room, and so did the girls. Mama stayed home and took care of us, while Dad worked at the hotel as a dishwasher. We had very little but there was always food on the table. I could see that Dad was bothered by what he couldn't provide. He started drinking. At first it was only on weekends. Then it got worse. Dad came home from work late. Mama always stayed up waiting for him. He was always falling over drunk. He blamed Mama for everything that went wrong and was physically abusive."

PSYCHIC CINDY: "Did anyone try to stop your dad?"

SCENE OF CASTRO FAMILY HOME 29 YEARS AGO, UPPER EAST SIDE

A tall man of 6-foot-4 is fumbling with his house keys trying to find the keyhole. As he makes his way into the apartment, he slams the door shut.

MR. CASRO: "Poonyetta, what the f**ck?"

MARIA: "Raul, please, the children are asleep. You were drinking?"

RAUL: "Maria, bitch! Shut up."

With his huge monster-size hands, Raul slaps his wife across the face. She falls against the wall to the floor. She holds her scream to avoid waking up the children. She sobs and shakes uncontrollably as she lays there.

RAUL: "Get me something to eat!!! Can't a man come home to a decent fu@king meal?"

Maria turns on the stove and finds a plate from the shelf. She is shaking and hoping that the food heats up fast. She wants him to eat so he can get sober quicker. With her hands shaking, Maria quickly gathers a plate of rice, beans, and chicken. She persuades Raul to sit at the table and eat.

RAUL: "How the hell can I pay these bills?"

MARIA: "Raul, please."

RAUL: "Why you look at me that way? Where is my favorite girl?"
Maria pretends that she doesn't understand him. She hopes he forgets and tries to change the subject.

MARIA: "Want something to drink?"

RAUL: "Are you crazy? Been freaking drinking all night! Where's my baby, Ramona?"

BACK TO PSYCHIC CINDY AND RAMONA

PSYCHIC CINDY: "Ramona, are you okay?"

DEMON JULIA: "It's me, Julia."

PSYCHIC CINDY: "Okay, Julia, this is not funny. I need to speak to Ramona."

DEMON JULIA: "Why do you need her?"

PSYCHIC CINDY: "She needs my help."

DEMON JULIA: "I'm not feeling too good myself."

PSYCHIC CINDY: "Tell me how come."

DEMON JULIA: "Just that I don't feel well."

PSYCHIC CINDY: "Why?"

DEMON JULIA: "Don't know why."

I suspected that Ramona was gaining strength, and this was making Demon Julia weak. All that was needed was to push Ramona further. She would no longer need Julia to escape from the trauma that she so deeply suppressed. I had a plan to push Ramona along, but I needed to use Julia to get my plan to work.

PSYCHIC CINDY: "Julia, I need your help."

DEMON JULIA: "You need my help?"

PSYCHIC CINDY: "Yes."

DEMON JULIA: "What do I get out of it? I like it here."

PSYCHIC CINDY: "You get to have me."

DEMON JULIA: "I get to have you?"

PSYCHIC CINDY: "You can enter me."

DEMON JULIA: "Oh, I get it."

Unknown to Demon Julia is that psychics are immune to identity disorders or spirits. They see spirits and are around them all the time. Spirits, demons, or angelic beings have no effect on them.

PSYCHIC CINDY: "You can stay with me as long as you like."

DEMON JULIA: "Deal. What do I have to do?"

PSYCHIC CINDY: "The next time I speak to Ramona, do not interfere. No matter what happens, do not come out. After you're out of her, you can have me."

DEMON JULIA: "Piece of cake. I'm going to enjoy being with you. I've never been inside a psychic."

PSYCHIC CINDY: "I guarantee it will be fun."

DEMON JULIA: "Okay! When can we start?"

FINAL SESSION, RAMONA AND PSYCHIC CINDY

PSYCHIC CINDY: "Ramona, I want to go back to when Father came home at night, okay?"

RAMONA: "Do we have to?"

PSYCHIC CINDY: "Yes. It's going to be all right, I promise you. The last time we talked, you said your father asked for you."

RAMONA: "My dad came into my room at night."

PSYCHIC CINDY: "Where was your mom?"

RAMONA: "My mom was asleep."

PSYCHIC CINDY: "What happened then?"

Ramona was struggling with every word. This was the point where she would normally black out and the demon would come out. I could feel the demon there but she was holding back, as she agreed.

RAMONA: "Daddy, no! Daddy, no! I'll be a good girl, Daddy, please. Get off of me please, Daddy! Get off."

SCANDALS

PSYCHIC CINDY: "Tell me, Ramona, what happened next? What did your dad do to you?"

RAMONA: "I asked him to stop. He wouldn't stop. He got on top of me. He raped me! He raped me! My daddy raped me. Daddy raped me."

I hugged Ramona and held on to her. As I held her in my arms, I rocked her back and forth like she was my own daughter. She continued to sob, but I felt no tightness in her body. The demon was nearby but unable to enter me or her. Ramona was going to be all right. Ramona had finally faced the terrible ordeal. The demon that held her soul captive was gone. **RAMONA:** "Why did he do this? I loved my dad."

PSYCHIC CINDY: "Your dad was a sick man, Ramona. Sometimes people get sick. Sometimes they hurt the ones they love. He can't hurt you anymore."

When Ramona left, she had a strange glow around her. I knew that our business was over and that I would not be seeing her again. I told Ramona that my door is always open to her. She is welcome to come back for any reason. She hugged and thanked me and, for the first time since we met, she stood a little taller.

A WEEK LATER AT THE OFFICE OF PSYCHIC CINDY

My next client was a repeat client name Rosie. She is a retired detective I've known for some time.

DETECTIVE ROSIE: "Hi, Cindy! Where have you been, girl?"

PSYCHIC CINDY: "Working with a client. Like always."

DETECTIVE ROSIE: "I called you several times, left you messages."

PSYCHIC CINDY: "I haven't checked my messages. Probably have eighty or more messages waiting."

DETECTIVE ROSIE: "I got the info you ask me for on that Ramona girl."

PSYCHIC CINDY: "That's the client I was with."

DETECTIVE ROSIE: "What? Impossible."

PSYCHIC CINDY: "What do you mean? I was with her for about a week."

DETECTIVE ROSIE: "But, Cindy, she's a DOA. She's been dead for two months!!!"

BIOGRAPHY:

Psychic Cindy was born and raised in Brooklyn, New York by her loving parents, and has one sister. She resides with her two children and has been cultivating her psychic gift for over 20 years.

PROFESSIONAL ACCOMPLISHMENTS: Over the years, Cindy has exploited her gift in various ways. As she discovered in her late teen years, she had the ability to envision events and results in the future as well as events that had occurred. She is not limited to just reading clients in today's world but can also communicate with those loved ones who have departed us. Her readings are genuine and leave her clients breathless and astonished at her abilities. She unselfishly helps those who seek out her assistance and becomes sincerely interested in their plights and aspirations. Often, a shimmer of hope is all a person needs to muster the strength to conquer their challenges, and Cindy has an impeccable 100% client satisfaction rating thus far.

Her assertiveness and tenacity to get at the truth has earned the respect of several NYPD detectives whom she has helped with several cases involving murder, kidnapping, child abuse and endangerment. Cindy was also a guest on CSI radio. Her credibility is impeccable!

Cindy's cooperative union with New Age Productions has enabled her to provide confidential readings to restaurant patrons in New Jersey and all five New York boroughs. Her work is not limited to adults and she truly cares about the direction of today's youth. She offers counseling services to teens on sensitive subjects such as sex and drugs, which often they are hesitant to share with their parents. She was at an event with the Rainbow Hopes Foundation that helps autistic children. Her high-spirited ability to reach out and communicate with these children energized them and has left an indelible memory in them. Her clientele lists runs the gamut of professional athletes, musical rappers, soap opera personalities and cast members from a popular HBO series. She reserves the right to protect the confidentiality of her clients.

SERVICES OFFERED

In addition to one-on-one readings, Psychic Cindy offers phone and picture readings, special oils which she prepares, herbs, and candles. She provides personal classes on love, prosperity, health, protection and self-improvement. In addition to cleansing baths, gift packages and money spells, she also offers gift angels and bracelets. She has authored two books and is currently working on a third. Psychic Cindy is truly an exceptional one of a kind and will amaze you with the powers of her gift!

In June 2008 Psychic Cindy opened C-Treg's Ltd Fashion and Accessories, & Greeting Cards for all Occasion's www.ctregs.com

Psychic Cindy has also done several fundraisers for New Jersey Fire Company's, Mylestone Esquire Horse Rescue, Charity Event helping raise Money for Cancer patients, and more.

Made in the USA
Columbia, SC
21 August 2018